Sir John Fortescue's
The Clasping of the Jewel

Sir John Fortescue's
The Clasping of the Jewel
The British Army and the Wars to Secure India
1840-1850

J. W. Fortescue

LEONAUR

Sir John Fortescue's The Clasping of the Jewel
The British Army and the Wars to Secure India 1840-1850
by J. W. Fortescue

FIRST EDITION

First published under the title
A History of the British Army Vol 12 (Account)

Leonaur is an imprint of Oakpast Ltd

Copyright in this form © 2015 Oakpast Ltd

ISBN: 978-1-78282-497-8 (hardcover)
ISBN: 978-1-78282-498-5 (softcover)

http://www.leonaur.com

Publisher's Notes

Contents

CHAPTER 1

Napier's Conquest of Sind

At the very end of 1841 there arrived at Bombay Major-General Charles Napier, who had been appointed through the Duke of Wellington to the staff of the Army in India. He assumed command of a brigade on the 28th of December, and in March 1842 was called upon by Lord Ellenborough, who had just received the news of the disaster at Kabul, to advise him as to the means of remedying it. Unfortunately the First Afghan War would prove to be irredeemable and had some of its course yet to run before it finally came to its unhappy conclusion.

In July he was appointed to the command of Upper and Lower Sind, his jurisdiction extending from the Khojak pass eastward to Sukkur and thence to the sea; and on the 3rd Sept. of September he sailed from Bombay for Karachi, where he arrived on the 9th after a terrible passage. For the steamer in which he travelled carried also two hundred British troops, of whom sixty-four died of cholera before the voyage was ended. He had received no instructions from Bombay; he was not even informed as to the number of troops that would be under him; but it was very evident that Ellenborough was apprehensive as to the attitude both of the Amirs of Sind and of the Sikhs, in view of the coming withdrawal of the troops from Afghanistan.

Sind, it must be remembered, was divided into three states, Khairpur or Upper Sind, Hyderabad or Lower Sind, and Mirpur, of which the principal *amirs* were named Rustam, Nasir Khan and Sher Mohamed, known as the Lion, respectively. Ascending the Indus, Napier visited the Amirs of Hyderabad, whom, having full political as well as military control, he rebuked for sundry violations of the treaty of 1839. Passing on to Sukkur, which he reached on the 5th of October, he there received intimation of the governor-general's policy. Ellenborough admitted that, looking to the treatment which they had received from Auckland, it was too much to expect the *amirs* to be friendly to the British. None the less he had to accept matters as he found them; and he gave distinct orders that if any of the *amirs* who had signed Auckland's treaty now evinced hostile intentions, they must be visited with signal punishment. It cannot be questioned that this dealt hard measure to the *amirs*; but the situation was in the highest degree critical. Quite apart from the safety of the troops retreating from Afghanistan, the posture of the Sikhs was extremely doubtful; and beyond these considerations there was the darling project of the East India Directors, the navigation of the Indus.

Very quickly Outram, who had been political resident in Sind, discovered and communicated to Napier evidence of hostile designs on the part of the *amirs*; and the general, reviewing the situation, recommended that the Indian government should annex Karachi, Sukkur, Bukkur and Sabzalcot, releasing the *amirs* in return from all tribute, and that a new treaty to that effect should be signed by them. Ellenborough agreed; two draft treaties for Khairpur and Hyderabad were sent to Napier, and were by him submitted to the two *amirs* at the end of November. He of Hyderabad professed obedience; Rustam also yielded, though under protest. Napier distrusted the promises of submission, feeling sure that the *amirs* designed to protract negotiations until the heat of summer should make military movements impossible. On the 8th of December he proclaimed the annexation of the country from Sabzalcot to Rohri; on the 16th he threw a strong force across the Indus, and in the next few days he occupied Sabzalcot. The younger *amirs*, indignant, half-frightened and half-bewildered at this summary procedure, gathered in recruits from their clans and made preparation for war.

Napier had at this time about eight thousand troops under his hand, including the five battalions of *sepoys* which had escorted England's column from Kandahar. But all the troops at Sukkur were miserably sickly. The barracks were low houses of mud, without windows, doors or proper means of ventilation; and four hundred men were packed, only four feet apart, in a long low room no more than twelve feet high. The air at night consequently became pestilential; and the men rose from their beds, bathed in sweat, and staggered out into the open air to sleep, where, of course, they caught chills and fevers. Such were the quarters of the British troops in Sind, where the thermometer in summer rises to one hundred and thirty degrees Fahrenheit; and those of the *sepoys* were even worse. Before the end of November Napier was fain to summon to him the Twenty-Second Foot from Karachi.

He still hoped to effect his purpose without bloodshed, and to that end succeeded in gaining over Ali Murad, the ablest of the Amirs of Upper Sind, to whom the unhappy Rustam, at the end of December, resigned his chiefship. Thereupon, the younger Amirs of Khairpur fled away with their followers; and it was said that they had taken refuge at the fortress of Imamgarh, which lay far away in the desert some eighty miles south-east of Khairpur. It occurred to Napier that the capture of this fortress would have a profound moral effect as proving that no stronghold, however remote or difficult of access, was safe from the invincible British troops, and so convincing the *amirs* of the hopelessness of resistance.

Having at the end of December established his camp near Khairpur he, on the 3rd of January 1843, moved one march southward to Diji Kot, where he learned that one only of the *amirs*, a nephew of Rustam, had gone to Imamgarh. None the less he persisted in his intention to show that he could go there himself. The enterprise was most hazardous, for he could get no certain information about the route or the watering-places. He had few camels except those that were already weakened by service in Afghanistan, and could not therefore take with him a large force; so he contented himself with three hundred and fifty men of the Twenty-Second mounted in pairs on camels, two hundred of the Sind Horse and two twenty-four-pounder howitzers.

With these, with water for four days and provisions for fifteen, at midnight on the 5th he plunged into the desert. On the first day he covered twenty-four miles, and on the five ensuing from ten to eleven, the labour of hauling the howitzers through the deep sand being very severe. He found abundance of water on the 6th, 7th and 9th, and reaching Imamgarh on the 12th found it evacuated. A vast quantity of powder had been abandoned in it, so Napier blew it up on the 15th, and, returning by a different route, halted on the 21st a short distance to south of Diji Kot. He had met with no resistance whatever, though he was prepared for it, and he was fortunate in finding Imamgarh deserted, for the place was very strong and stoutly built, and he might not have found it easy to batter a practicable breach with the supply of ammunition that he carried with him.

The Duke of Wellington described the operation as one of the most curious military feats that he had ever heard or read of, and, though the British have fought more than one desert campaign since

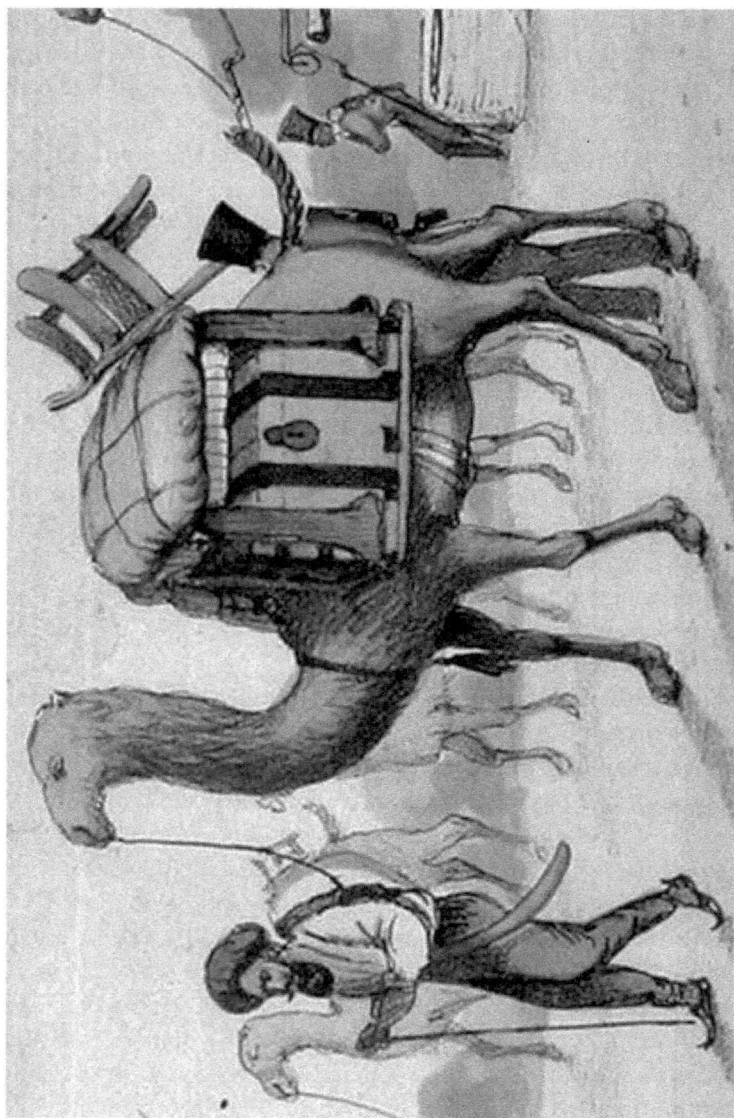

those days, it remains remarkable. Whether it were worth the risk is another matter. Napier certainly believed that it was, and undertook it with the sincere intention of averting bloodshed.

The negotiations were then resumed, Outram, of whom Napier had then a high opinion, having started on the 5th to meet the *amirs* or their ambassadors at Khairpur. He saw Rustam on his way, and found the old man full of despair and of mistrust which he was unable to dispel. He reached Khairpur on the 20th and met ambassadors from Lower Sind, but not Rustam, nor any from Upper Sind. Looking into the terms of the treaty, he judged them to be unreasonably harsh, and warned Napier that, if they were insisted upon, no satisfactory settlement could be expected. Returning to the subject, he wrote again condemning the proposed measures as "most tyrannical—positive robbery," his conclusion was such:

I consider that every life that may hereafter be lost in consequence will be a murder.

Napier was impatient of any opinion that coincided not with his own. He had so far admired Outram, and had christened him the Bayard of India. He was very shortly to fail to find epithets strong enough to express his hatred and contempt of him.

Meanwhile, Napier had begun on the 27th to move slowly southward upon Hyderabad, whither the Amirs of Upper Sind, with four thousand armed men, were moving to claim the help of their brethren in Lower Sind. Outram begged Napier for leave to go there likewise, hoping to dissuade those of Lower Sind from receiving them; but the general refused his permission for six days, and the letter in which at last he granted it was intercepted. On the 30th envoys from Hyderabad came to Napier's camp about fifty miles southwest of Khairpur, and were informed that, unless they induced the Amirs of Khairpur to meet Outram at Hyderabad by the 5th of February, the general would treat those *amirs* as enemies.

Napier was in fact impatient lest the hot weather should come upon him while matters were still unsettled; and the *amirs* construed this impatience as determination to fight. Outram, arriving at Hyderabad on the 8th, strove still to avert war, and Napier, who had resumed his march southward on the 6th, twice halted in deference to his entreaties, though he was convinced that Outram was being fooled. So anxious, indeed, was he for Outram's safety that on the 11th he sent a company of the Twenty-Second to the Residency at Hyderabad.

GENERAL SIR CHARLES NAPIER, OF SIND, CALLED BY THE NATIVES "SHAYTÁN KÁ BHÁI."

On the 12th Outram had another conference with the *amirs*, and at its close was threatened by a furious mob without. The *amirs*, confessing that they could no longer restrain their people, begged him to leave the city; but he lingered until the 15th, still vainly hoping to maintain peace, when the Residency was attacked by eight thousand Baluchis, and, after a gallant defence of four hours, he was compelled to withdraw his little garrison to a steamer that was under his orders, and return with them up the Indus to Napier.

He overtook him, on the 16th, at Matiari, some twenty miles above Hyderabad, and found him resolved, with good reason, to fight, for he had intercepted a letter from one of the Amirs of Lower Sind calling upon all clansmen to assemble at Miani, ten miles north of Hyderabad, and a day's march from Matiari. Napier's information was that he would find thirty thousand men collected there to oppose him; and he himself had three thousand only. Yet he never dreamed of shrinking from a battle, having taken to heart Wellington's maxim that one must never retreat before an Oriental enemy. Outram, eager to take his share in the fight now that it was inevitable, asked for a detachment to move with him down the river again and set fire to the forests that lined the road to Miani, for the protection of the general's march. Napier consented, and in the afternoon Outram dropped down stream with two hundred convalescent *sepoys*. But the *amirs*, having information of his plan, shifted their forces eight miles to the east, and the firing of the woods accomplished nothing.

At four o'clock on the morning of the 17th, Napier set his little force in motion. He had with him the Sind Horse under Captain John Jacob, the Poona Horse and the Ninth Bengal Cavalry, together about eight hundred strong, the Twenty-Second Foot, about five hundred bayonets, the First Bombay Grenadiers, Twelfth and Twenty-Fifth Bombay Infantry, (these last two had formed part of England's column), each of them between four and five hundred bayonets, and twelve guns, mostly drawn by camels.

The way lay along a level plain intersected by dry water-courses; and, as it was necessary to level these for the camel-teams, progress was very slow. Hence it was not until seven o'clock, after a march of seven miles, that the Sind Horse and the Madras Sappers and Miners which, with two guns, formed the vanguard, reached the dry bed of the River Fuleli, running east of them and parallel to the line of advance. Here the sound of cannon was heard; and Napier, halting the Sappers, pushed forward the Sind Horse to explore both banks of the

Battle of Meeanee

river. They reported the enemy to be in front; and Napier, moving on with the vanguard, came at about eight o'clock within sight of the enemy's camp. Ascending a hillock, the general could make out on his right front a large wood bounded by a high wall, on which were perched hundreds of matchlock men, and on the left front a grove of mango-trees. In the space of about twelve hundred yards between these two were the enemy's guns irregularly drawn up to cover their flanks, and behind them could be seen bodies of horse in movement, masses of foot, and, in rear of all, the encampment.

Napier now halted to await the main column, which had been delayed by the bad condition of the road, sending Captain John Jacob with the Sind Horse round to explore the ground on the left of the enemy's position. To turn the wood on the right would be difficult, for the troops would have to cross the Fuleli under the enemy's fire, and would then have to clear the jungle. Their formation must inevitably be destroyed, and being young soldiers, unused to woodland fighting, they would infallibly shoot each other.

Either, therefore, he must turn the left of the *amirs*, or make a frontal attack on a re-entrant angle; and what the re-entrant angle might contain it was impossible to discover, for the Baluchi artillery forbade the cavalry to come within five hundred yards of it. Advancing to within three hundred yards of the wood, Napier deployed, with the Madras Sappers on the extreme right, then his twelve guns, and then in succession the Twenty-Second, the Twenty-Fifth and Twelfth Bombay Infantry and the First Bombay Grenadiers, the Sind Horse taking the extreme left. In rear of the right the Ninth Bombay Cavalry were held in reserve.

The line remained halted in this formation, pending Jacob's return, and meanwhile a few skirmishers were sent forward to clear the matchlock-men from the wall. Napier noticed that the latter disappeared completely, and drew the inference that they had made no loopholes nor *banquette* to enable them to fire through or over the wall, so that his right flank might be so far protected. On the other hand, he now perceived that there was a village in the mango-trees on his left, which made that point the more formidable against attack. The enemy's guns kept up a desultory cannonade during this interval, but the range, about a thousand yards, was too great for them, and the shot fell harmless before the feet of the general and his staff. At length Jacob rode up and made his report.

On the further side of the village there was a deep ravine with

Captain John Jacob with the Sind Horse

scarped sides, strongly occupied by the enemy and virtually impassable. There was nothing left but to deliver a frontal attack, and, to all intent, to force the passage of a defile with some twenty-eight hundred men against thirty thousand.

At about half-past ten Napier began his advance, pushing his guns forward until they had silenced the hostile artillery, while the infantry followed in echelon of battalions from the right, the left being refused in view of the greater menace of a flank attack from the village.

Moreover, riding by the wall of the wood on the right the general noticed an opening, not very wide, which he promptly closed with the grenadier company of the Twenty-Second under Captain Tew, placing the men just within the wood with orders to block the entrance, if necessary, until the last man should have fallen. Then halting the echelon and dressing the battalions in order to steady his young soldiers, he parked his baggage in a circle, the camels lying down with heads inward, and with bales between their bodies, to form a defensible rampart. Four companies of *sepoys* and the Poona Horse were told off as baggage-guard, and with the remnant, about two thousand of all ranks, Napier advanced to the attack.

The enemy abandoned their guns as the Twenty-Second approached, though the echelon encountered a galling fire of matchlock-men; but the onward movement was proceeding steadily, when Napier suddenly perceived, three hundred yards ahead of him, a row of dark faces just showing above the level of the plain. Then he realised that he had utterly mistaken the situation. The Baluchi horse and foot that he had seen were the enemy's reserves; and their main body was ensconced in the bed of the Fuleli, which, unknown to him, made a sudden bend at right angles to his front. The guns were brought forward and unlimbered within a few feet of the bank, but, owing to an outward turn of the wall, there was no room for more than four out of the twelve to come into action, and the remaining eight, together with the Madras Sappers, were crowded out of the line.

The infantry advanced steadily, and Napier, waiting for the right moment, gave the word to charge. The Twenty-Second dashed forward with a shout, reached the edge of the bank and stopped abruptly. The river-bed was one sea of fierce faces and gleaming swords, and they hesitated to engulf themselves within it. For a short time they stood their ground and poured in volley after volley; but they began to drop fast under the fire of the Baluchi matchlock-men, and presently they shrank back eight or ten paces and would come forward no more.

Their officers, by example and entreaty, did their utmost to make them charge again. Lieutenant McMurdo leaped down into the river-bed alone and killed four of the enemy with his own hand, but still the men would not charge. They were quite right. If they had leaped into that host of savage men to fight hand to hand, they would have been swallowed up by numbers. By drawing back only for ten yards they were sheltered from the whole of the Baluchi fire except that of the men who lined the bank, and by advancing to fire and retiring again to load they inflicted much damage and received very little. The *sepoys* on their left followed their example, and so the fight was maintained. Napier and his staff still called on the men to charge, and at length the Twenty-Second cried out, "Mr. McMurdo, if you don't leave off, we'll shoot you."

Napier himself rode slowly up and down between the opposing arrays, pouring out torrents of blasphemous exhortation, so close to both sides that he was actually singed by the powder, and yet by some miracle unscathed by either. His appearance was so strange that the Baluchis might well have mistaken him for a demon. Beneath a huge helmet of his own contrivance there issued a fringe of long hair at the back, and in front a large pair of round spectacles, an immense hooked nose, and a mane of moustache and whisker reaching to the waist. But though the opposing arrays were not ten yards apart, neither he nor his horse were touched. From time to time the Baluchis made furious counter-attacks in small bodies.

Some chief called upon his clansmen, and they stormed forward, irresistible, bearing the *sepoys* back; but, being only a few, their flanks were riddled and shattered before they could drive their charge home. Had they made such an onslaught from end to end of the line, they must have carried everything before them. Had they fallen upon the guns, they must inevitably have captured them. But they were an assembly of tribes and not an army, under the direction of a score of chiefs and not of one, and Napier's cannon swept their masses with enfilading fire of grape unchecked and unmolested.

Meanwhile, the British soldiers warmed to their work. At first some of them had fired wildly and high, scorching Napier's huge whiskers. Now they came forward three or four at a time in quick succession, fired and went back to reload, before they could be fired at themselves. They thus crushed the matchlock-men of the Baluchi front rank out of existence, and shot down those who would have taken their place before they could reach it. Still the enemy would not give way; and their right was little troubled because the officer in command of the Bombay Grenadiers, evidently an unintelligent person, kept his men back, so as to preserve the echelon formation originally prescribed to him. Jacob, after a bold effort to turn the grove on that flank, had returned to report that he could not pass the deep *nullah*. Napier perceived that it was time for decisive action, and ordered the whole of his cavalry to charge the Baluchis' right flank.

Passing in single file between the grenadiers and the village, two squadrons of the Ninth Light Cavalry cleared the enclosures about the houses, and swept down upon the river-bed, while another squadron, crossing it, fell upon the front, and the Sind Horse upon the flank, of the Baluchi reserves. The enemy in the river-bed wavered; Napier's infantry sprang down among them; and, meanwhile, the Sappers having made a breach in the wall, a gun was pointed through it which quickly swept the wood clear with grape. But still the Baluchis fought on, and when at last they gave up the struggle in the river-bed, they fled not, but stalked slowly away. Napier, however, was now able to bring the whole of his guns into action; the last groups were thus broken up; and the field was won.

The fight had lasted for four hours, and in that time some two thousand Baluchis had fallen. Four hundred corpses alone were heaped up within a circle of fifty yards' radius. In Napier's force there fell sixty-four of all ranks killed and one hundred and ninety-four wounded, the share of the Twenty-Second being one officer and twenty-three men killed, six officers and fifty-two men wounded. In the circumstances the casualties of the British cannot be considered heavy, for, beyond all question, they walked straight into a trap. How far Napier was to blame for this, it is not easy to say. It seems strange that no guide should have told him of the course of the Fuleli; and considering that he mistook the reserves of the Baluchis for their front line, it is not quite clear why a staff officer or two, or even a line of skirmishers, should not have been pushed forward to examine the ground over which he purposed to advance.

But it is not difficult to be wise after the event; and, since Napier by sheer tenacity overcame all difficulties, it would be churlish to grudge him his meed of praise. Confronted with a most disconcerting surprise at a time when he had already committed himself beyond recall to a certain plan of action, he was not for a moment dismayed, but carried that plan through with inflexible determination. Never was there a more signal instance of the triumph of what is called the will to victory. On the other hand, it is remarkable that such a veteran should have chosen the wrong tactics for the fighting of the battle, and that his young soldiers, who had never seen a shot fired, should instinctively have chosen the right and stuck to them in defiance of all commands.

Napier encamped for the night on the plain beyond the Fuleli; and in the morning emissaries arrived to ask him what terms he would grant the *amirs*. "Life, and nothing more," he answered, "and I require your decision before noon." Presently three Amirs of Hyderabad arrived, gave up their swords and promised to surrender the fortress of Hyderabad. On the 19th two more *amirs* from Khairpur gave in their submission, and Sher Mohamed, Amir of Mirpur, known as the Lion, who had been encamped with ten thousand men only six miles from Miani during the battle, likewise sent a friendly message. By Outram's advice Napier answered that, if the Lion disbanded his troops, he should be treated as a friend or ally.

On the 19th the British marched into Hyderabad; two more *amirs*, who had failed to yield themselves up, were made prisoners; and all, outwardly, seemed to be well. But in truth Napier was uneasy, and with good reason. His force was seriously diminished; the Lion, far from dispersing his followers, was assiduously gathering in recruits; the sun was daily waxing in strength, which signified increase of sickness among the Europeans; and it was useless to march against the Lion who, even if defeated, could always take refuge in the desert. He therefore resolved to stand fast, threw up an entrenched camp on the east bank of the Indus, near Hyderabad, and wrote both to Sukkur and Karachi to summon reinforcements.

Swiftly the plot thickened. The wild hill-tribes to west of the Indus were preparing to descend upon the plains, greedy of plunder, and Karachi itself was threatened by the most powerful chief in Southern Sind. By the second week in March the Lion's following exceeded five and twenty thousand men, and Napier, on the 13th, summoned further reinforcements from Ferozepore. Ellenborough, however, had of himself ordered a brigade from that place to Sukkur, whither Colonel Roberts, the commandant, who had already despatched troops by water in response to Napier's first appeal, now sent a battalion of infantry, a regiment of cavalry and five guns by land, under command of Major Stack.

On the 15th the Lion advanced to within twelve miles of Hydera-

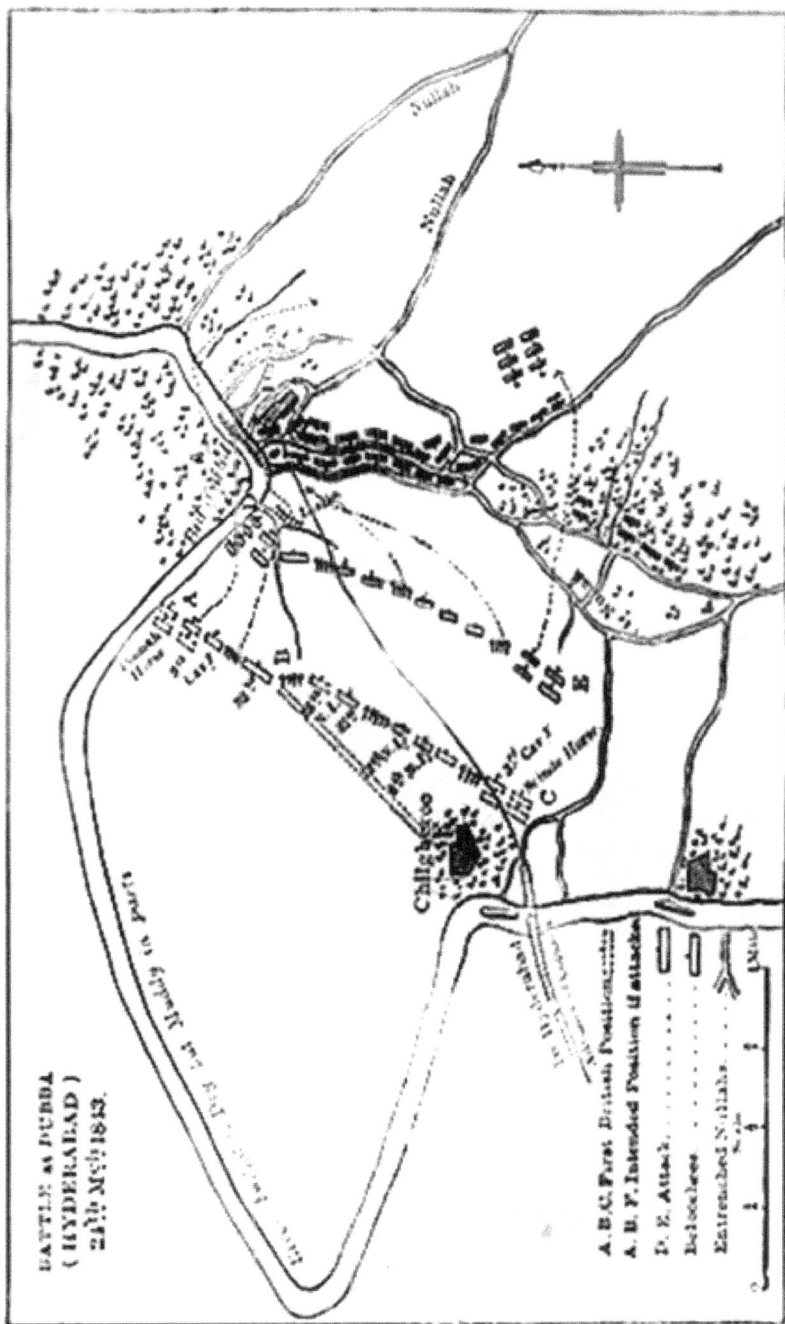

BATTLE at DUBBA (HYDERABAD) 24th March 1843.

A.B.C. First British Positions...........
A.B.F. Intended Position of attack.....
P.E. Attack......................
Enfeladees....................
Entrenched Nullah..............

bad and sent envoys to propose terms to Napier. These arrived just upon the firing of the evening gun, which, the general told them, they might take for their answer. None the less he was extremely anxious lest Stack might be intercepted; but Sher Mohamed did not attack Stack's column until it was within five miles of Hyderabad, and then so unskilfully that he was with little difficulty repulsed. By midnight of the 22nd Stack had brought his brigade safely into Napier's camp.

On the forenoon of the 23rd, by a remarkable coincidence, the reinforcements from Sukkur and Karachi arrived simultaneously from up and down stream, raising Napier's force to five thousand men. The rest of the day was spent in active preparation, and early on the 24th he marched out northward with the regiments that had fought at Miani, also the Eighth and Twenty-First Bombay Infantry, the Third Bengal Cavalry and five additional guns. His direction was upon Khuseri, where the Lion was reported to lie. After travelling four miles Napier learned from a peasant that the enemy had moved further to east, and, altering his course accordingly, he sent the Sind Horse forward to reconnoitre. At 8 a.m. a trooper rode in with the news that the entire army of the Lion was drawn up at Dabo only two miles away. Napier galloped forward to see for himself, but could make out remarkably little. There were two woods a mile apart, which seemed to be the right and left of the enemy's position. About the right centre was a grove of trees which was conjectured to conceal a village, though no houses were to be perceived; and, in rear of what Napier judged to be the Baluchi left, were visible great masses of horse.

Closer reconnaissance of the front of this position was impossible except through an actual attack, but examination of the enemy's right flank showed that it rested on the Fuleli, which, dry elsewhere, was at this point a half-dried water-hole of deep soft mud. This obstacle banished all ideas of an assault upon that flank; and the wood beside the river was found to extend so far to the enemy's rear as to prohibit any but a very wide turning movement. Furthermore, the approach to the enemy's line was contracted, for it lay across the Fuleli, through a kind of defile formed by a network of ravines; and the bed of the river made a great loop, which practically would enclose the whole rear of the British after the defile was passed. In fact, the ground was awkward and cramped, full of dangerous possibilities in the event of a mishap.

So much Napier could mark with his own eyes. What he could not see was something far more formidable. Along the whole length of the line ran two parallel water-courses, the foremost twenty feet wide and eight feet deep, the rearward forty-two feet wide and seventeen feet deep, both of which had been scarped to form a parapet, with one or two ramps prepared for advance or retreat. In these watercourses were ensconced the first and second lines of Baluchi infantry with their guns posted behind them. On the right Baluchi flank the village of Dabo, of which Napier could see nothing, was filled with men, the houses being loop-holed and prepared for defence. And the Baluchi line did not end, as Napier supposed, with the wood on their left; but a water-course, which likewise had been scarped and strengthened, ran back for half a mile at an obtuse angle from the ravines in front; and this was the true left of their array. Moreover, the enemy had formed yet another line of resistance in ravines some distance in rear of their main position. Altogether they had chosen their ground well, and developed its advantages with admirable skill.

The course of the British march led the head of the column in a direction diagonal to the hostile line; and Napier deployed upon this same alignment, with his cavalry on either flank and his guns in the intervals between battalions, the Twenty-Second forming the extreme left of his infantry. Having been warned by spies that the Baluchis had selected five thousand of their choicest warriors to assail him as soon as he should attack, he conjectured that this onslaught would probably be delivered from the wood on his right, and he accordingly pushed forward the cavalry on that wing under Major Stack, to gain himself time enough for changing front to meet it.

Meanwhile, his deployment was hardly completed before the enemy's cannon, opening with effect upon his left wing, compelled him to draw it back out of range Then Lieutenant Waddington, of the Engineers, with two more officers, rode coolly close up to the centre of the Baluchi position and thence towards its right, drawing a heavy fusillade of matchlock-men and thus revealing the first ravine of the enemy's right centre, though not the second, nor the prolongation of their line beyond the wood on their left. Napier was still greatly in the dark as to what might lie before him, when a sudden movement of the enemy precipitated him into action.

Large bodies of the Baluchis were all at once observed hurrying from their left towards Dabo. Napier, supposing that they had neglected to occupy that village and were hastening to repair the blunder, decided that he would be beforehand with them, and set his troops in motion. Major Leslie's troop of horse-artillery, supported by the cavalry of the left wing, advanced first, diagonally, to gain the extreme right of the Baluchi line where it rested on the Fuleli, unlimbering and firing from time to time as it went forward. This movement caused the enemy to betray the whole length of their position, and Leslie was able to enfilade their hitherto concealed left wing from end to end.

★★★★★★

So says William Napier; but, if his account of the extent of the Baluchi line be correct, the range must have been very long for round shot, and impossible for grape. Possibly Leslie fired shrapnel, but for this he would need howitzers, and there was only one howitzer to each battery. I confess that I am puzzled by this detail.

★★★★★★

The two remaining batteries likewise advanced in succession and took up raking positions to cross their fire with that of Leslie. Meanwhile the infantry also was on march in echelon of battalions from the left, the Twenty-Second leading; and the Twenty-Second's light company on the extreme left suffered heavily from the fire of matchlockmen and from a single gun on a hillock midway between the two ravines. Napier was himself about to lead a charge of the infantry on his left, when a messenger galloped up to tell him that his cavalry on the right was charging. Stack, seeing numbers of Baluchis hurrying in apparent confusion from their left towards their centre, had concluded that they were smitten with panic, and that such an opportunity was not to be missed. Realising that his right flank was now uncovered, Napier committed the attack of the Twenty-Second to Major Poole and spurred at the top of his speed to the other end of the line.

There he could see Stack's horsemen galloping across the *nullahs*, shouting and waving their swords in mad career; and he knew at once with indignation that they had passed beyond his control. There was nothing to be done except to leave his right flank to chance; and racing back to the extreme left he overtook the Twenty-Second on the brink of the first ravine, and called to them to charge. Without hesitation the men plunged down into the midst of the Baluchi swordsmen, and, seconded by Leslie's guns, made havoc of them with bullet and bayonet, till they drove them into the second ravine.

The Twenty-Fifth Native Infantry presently came into action on their right and the two forced their way across the second ravine and fell upon Dabo, which was strongly held. The cavalry, and Leslie's battery worked their way round the village, partly in the bed of the Fuleli, partly in the track of the infantry, and cut it off; and the rest of the line of infantry, witnessing the victory of Stack's cavalry, swiftly crossed the two ravines, and, bringing up their right shoulders, surrounded the village completely.

Napier, having forced his way through it, put himself at the head of the Bengal Cavalry and the Poona Horse, led the pursuit in person on his left wing and hunted the enemy for several miles; but on the right Colonel Patch arrested the chase just when the capture of the Lion in person seemed certain. This was unfortunate, though not perhaps unreasonable, for Stacks troopers had been galloping for about a couple of hours and must have been dispersed in all directions; and, though the Baluchi horse took to flight, the Baluchi swordsmen fought hard to the last. But for the escape of the hostile leader, the victory was sufficiently complete.

Such was the action which is generally known by the name of Hyderabad. The details are exceedingly obscure, but it should seem that the Baluchi left, which Napier so greatly dreaded, was unsteady from the very first. Apparently the British had hardly ranged themselves for battle before the enemy began to stream over from the left towards Dabo, and deluded Napier, pardonably enough, into his assault upon the enemy's right. This movement from their left continued, and Stack was probably correct in construing it as a panic. A host of mutually mistrustful tribes need only the withdrawal of one from the line of battle to make the remainder suspect treachery and withdraw likewise.

It is even possible that by accident or design the Lion posted the clans from the west of the Indus as far as possible from the river, and that they, or some of them, became suspicious on that very account. It is in any case certain that, except on their extreme right, the resistance of the Baluchis was poor. Napier's casualties did not exceed two hundred and seventy of all ranks, of which number twenty-three killed and one hundred and thirty-nine wounded belonged to the Twenty-Second; and the greater part of this loss was incurred in the storming of Dabo, which, as matters turned out, was quite unnecessary.

Napier, rightly commending troops which had fought splendidly for him, attributed his success to the Twenty-Second, and the artillery. The man who contributed most to it, as it should seem, was Stack, whom he blamed. Stack evidently swept away the Baluchi left, or such part of it as had not voluntarily decamped; and had Napier grasped this, he might have turned the Baluchi position by its left with the infantry on his own right, come in upon the flank of the two ravines, cleared them and battered the houses of Dabo to pieces with his artillery. But setting aside such easy wisdom after the event, it is plain that the Baluchis did not fight as well at Hyderabad as at Miani, though their losses were at least twice as heavy.

Halting for only eight hours after the battle, Napier moved eastward upon Mirpur, which surrendered on the 26th upon the appearance of the Poona Horse; the Lion having fled to Umarcot, sixty miles further to east. Dreading lest the inundation of the Indus should rise in his rear Napier kept his main force at Mirpur, and detached the Sind Horse and a camel battery to Umarcot, which defied them for a time, but on the flight of the Lion opened its gates on the 4th of April. There now remained to the fugitive April, chieftain one refuge, the fort of Shahgarh, in the desert, some sixty miles north-east of Imamgarh. To cut him off from this stronghold Napier posted a detachment at Rohri, and, to prevent his flight to the delta of the Indus, other troops were posted at Umarcot, Mirpur and Ali Ka Tanda. The heat was now intense and daily increasing, but none the less, in the course of the ensuing weeks, Napier drew his net closer and closer round. The marches were made, of course, by night, the men remaining by day in their tents, with wet cloths round their heads; but even so the deaths from heat-apoplexy were many.

On the 14th of June Napier himself was struck down, though he quickly recovered, but at the same time thirty-three Europeans fell in quick succession near him, of whom every one died within three hours. On that same day the Lion made a last desperate attempt upon a column under Colonel Jacob, who beat him off without losing a man. The Lion fled with only ten followers; and the conquest of Sind was at last accomplished.

There can be no question but that this was a great military achievement and of the first importance in restoring the prestige of the British in India. It was possible only for a commander who had the strength and ability at once to take great risks, and yet, so far as possible, to leave nothing to chance. Napier was hampered from the very first by lack of transport. The inference that he drew from this fact was not that his task was impracticable, but that it must be achieved by such a force as his limited amount of carriage permitted him to take into the field. Meanwhile, his transport must be made to go as far as possible, first by cutting down baggage to the lowest possible amount, and secondly by attention to the proper care and nourishment of the animals. The former of these requirements was easily achieved through the signal example set by himself, most frugal and self-denying of men in the matter of physical comfort.

The latter must have called for incessant personal watchfulness and activity. He speaks occasionally in his journal of the anxiety caused to him by his baggage, and of the small mortality among his camels; but of the means whereby he substituted good husbandry for the careless wastefulness which was the old tradition of the Indian Commissariat, he says little. Yet he did banish that evil tradition within a few weeks, and instilled a new and nobler spirit into all ranks of his little army, not merely by issuing orders, not merely by enforcing them ruthlessly when issued, but by sheer personal influence and personal inspiration.

Charles Napier was a curious compound of vanity and modesty with strange alternations of self-exaltation and self-abasement, but he possessed a power of intuition which guided him to the heart of things. He saw facts as they were clearly, he reasoned from them logically, and, having once framed his decision, he abode by it with inflexible will and indomitable courage, feeling confidence in himself and filling all about him with that confidence. There were doubtless officers who dreaded the sudden appearance of that uncouth figure, who seemed to be everywhere and carried with him always a piercing eye and a very caustic tongue. But the young and the keen—and there were not a few who would and did engage any number of enemies single-handed—welcomed his presence, for they felt that they could not do too much for him.

Above all, the private soldier knew him as his friend; and it was no mere accident that made Charles Napier the first general to mention the names of private soldiers in his despatches. So, too, it was no mere coincidence that ten men of the Twenty-Second, wounded at the Battle of Hyderabad, concealed their hurts and marched off—one of them even with a bullet in his foot—with their regiment next day. It was the personality of Charles Napier which evoked this spirit. His fame rests upon the two actions which he fought in Sind; but their success was due less to any tactical skill than to the magic of his leadership. He had never before commanded more than a battalion in action, and his troops, for the most part, had never seen a shot fired in anger. The military atmosphere in India was heavy with the disaster and disgrace of Afghanistan; and yet this untried general and his untried troops never hesitated to march into a re-entrant angle or to the attack of a fierce enemy which outnumbered them by ten or fifteen to one. It is no ordinary commander who can perform such miracles.

CHAPTER 2

The Troubles in Gwalior

After the conclusion of operations in China Hugh Gough returned to India by way of Calcutta to Madras, from whence he prepared to return to England. The chief command at Madras had actually been given to him, but had been withdrawn, since the government had decided that the functions of governor and commander-in-chief should be united in a single person. He was, however, compensated in May by his appointment to be commander-in-chief in India upon the retirement of Sir Jasper Nicolls; and to him, therefore, it fell to deal, apart from Scinde, with the aftermath of troubles which followed upon the Afghan War.

The first of these arose in the dominions of the Mahratta Chief, Scindia of Gwalior, upon the death of the Maharajah Jankoji Rao Scindia in February 1843. Jankoji, a worthless character, left no heir; and his widow, the Rani Tara Bai, a girl of twelve, adopted a boy, four years younger than herself, who was nearest in blood to Jankoji, as his successor. Meanwhile an uncle of Jankoji, known as Mama Sahib, was chosen as regent; and the governor-general, Ellenborough, signifying his approval of all these proceedings, declared himself prepared to support Mama Sahib's authority. Thereby, not unconsciously, he committed himself to, at least, the possibility of armed intervention. It was rare for one oriental ruler to succeed another without disturbance of some kind, and in this case the danger of trouble was aggravated by the fact that Scindia's Army was in arrears of pay, and a part of it at least in open mutiny.

For a few weeks all was quiet at Gwalior, and then, as usual, began intrigues of court and *harem*. A faction arose under the leadership of a late minister of the deceased Jankoji, one Dhada Khasji; and the Rani, from whatever cause, threw her influence on his side and gave him money to pay the mutinous troops. With the army at his back Dhada, after considerable riot and bloodshed, forced Mama Sahib to fly from Gwalior, and by the end of May reigned practically supreme. He then restored to office sundry persons who had been displaced by Jankoji on the representation of the Indian government, on account of their hostility to the British, and finally ordered the British Resident to remove from Gwalior to Dholpur, north of the Chambal, outside Scindia's dominions.

Ellenborough, who had moved up to Agra in the spring so as to be near at hand in case of trouble, decided in the middle of August to form an army of observation, twelve thousand strong, at that place, and summoned Gough to move up to Cawnpore. In September complications in the Punjab necessitated the strengthening of the British troops on the Sikh frontier, and diverted the attention of the commander-in-chief to that quarter; but in October he formed his plan of campaign in the event of further trouble at Gwalior. Deliberately and of set purpose defying the rules of strategy, he decided to divide his force, about twenty thousand men in all, into two parts, of which the right wing under his own command should move southward upon Gwalior from Agra, and the left wing, under Sir John Grey, north-westward from Bundelkhand.

The hostile army was reckoned at twenty-two thousand good troops, trained in the past by European officers (though none of these were now present), with three hundred guns; but the political officers, upon whom, as usual, sole dependence was placed for information, reported that this host was no more than a leaderless mob, whose heads were at variance with each other. In the circumstances Gough decided that either wing would suffice to overthrow any force that might encounter it, and that the approach of both from opposite directions would prevent the enemy from dispersing, after defeat, into gangs of *banditti*. The experience of Hastings in 1819 hardly confirmed this latter anticipation; but Gough was at least justified by the event.

By the beginning of December the right wing was assembling at Agra, and Gough had established a bridge of boats at Dholpur for the maintenance of his communications across the Chambal. The left wing was parted into two divisions at Kunch, about seventy miles east of Gwalior, and at Jhansi, about fifty miles south and west of Kunch, which two were to unite for the passage of the Sind at Seondha. But hostilities had not yet begun, nor seemed likely to begin. A counter-revolution at Gwalior in November had resulted in the fall and im-

Viscount Gough

prisonment of Dhada Khasji; and all that remained was that he should be delivered into the hands of the British.

Ellenborough arrived at Agra on the 11th of December, and gave orders for the two wings to advance upon the Chambal and the Sind; Gough's force being timed to be ready to cross at Dholpur on the 22nd, and Grey's two brigades to unite at Seondha on the same day. The threatening movement fulfilled its purpose, and on the 18th Dhada Khasji was surrendered into Ellenborough's hands. The governor-general then thought fit to require the reduction of the Gwalior Army, and as a means to that end ordered a further advance. He gave out, no doubt in good faith, that his object was the maintenance of peace, and he had no misgivings that the march would be more than a military promenade.

On the 22nd accordingly the right wing crossed the Chambal, and on the 24th the left wing crossed the Sind. By the 25th Grey had moved one day's march within Scindia's territory, and Gough was near Hingona, on the Kunwari River. Ellenborough was with him, awaiting a visit from the Rani of Gwalior on the morrow, and so confident of a peaceful issue that he had invited Lady Gough and her daughter to dine with him at Hingona. Another lady, familiar with active service, Mrs. Harry Smith, was also of the party; and there was eating and drinking on that Christmas Day.

But merriment there was not, for news came in that the *rani*, whether by her own will, or through constraint of her troops, would not meet the governor-general, but that, on the contrary, a large force, with artillery, had marched out from Gwalior some eleven miles north-westward on the road to Dholpur.

Plainly this signified war, and Gough therefore sent his final instructions to Grey, namely, that he should avoid the dangerous defile of Antri, on the direct road from Jhansi to Gwalior, turn westward till he struck the road leading from Narwar to the same capital, and follow it to Panniar. Gough reckoned that Grey should reach Panniar by the 30th, and ordered a detachment which lay at Sipri, some twenty miles south-west of Narwar, to join him there. Further co-operation between the two main forces of the British must depend upon circumstances; but it was evident that Gough must fight his way to Grey, for on the 26th it was known that the enemy had advanced seven miles further on the road to Dholpur, and had taken up a strong position at Chonda on the River Asan.

Gough at once sent out staff officers to reconnoitre this position, and Harry Smith, accompanying them on the 28th, drew up his report. Its purport was that the Mahrattas appeared to be about ten thousand strong, with several guns; that they were posted on difficult ground, with their left on the Asan and their right unprotected, as if they looked for the arrival of more troops; that the British ought to move up over against them without delay, and either await Grey's co-operation or attack them on the following morning. Gough decided upon immediate attack, and on the evening of the 28th issued his orders accordingly.

The distance to be traversed was about eight miles, beginning with the passage of the Kunwari River, and continuing over very rough and difficult country, much intersected by deep ravines, which were only made practicable by the work of the sappers. Gough had in all one British regiment of cavalry—the Sixteenth Lancers—four native regiments, and three troops of horse-artillery, two British battalions, the Thirty-Ninth and Fortieth, six native battalions, and two light field-batteries; in all about thirteen hundred and fifty horse, about four thousand eight hundred foot, and three hundred and fifty artillery with thirty light guns.

These he distributed into three columns. The right column, under Major-General Sir Joseph Thackwell, consisted of the Sixteenth Lancers, the governor-general's bodyguard, and two regiments of native cavalry; the centre column, under Major-general Valiant, of the Fortieth, and two native battalions; and the left column of the remainder of the force under Gough himself. (See list following)

★★★★★★

Right Column:
Thackwell. Cureton's brigade: 16th Lancers, Gov.-gen.'s bodyguard, 1st Bengal L.C., 4th Irregular Cav., Lane's and Alexander's troops of Horse Artillery.

Central Column:
Valiant. H.M. 40th, 2nd and 16th Bengal N.I.

Left Column:
Dennis's Infantry Div.; 14th, 31st and 43rd N.I., Browne's Light Field Battery.
Littler's Infantry Div.; H.M. 39th; 56th N.I., Saunders's Light Field Battery.
Scott's Cavalry Brigade; 4th and 10th Bengal L.C., Grant's troop H.A.

His plan was to fall upon and turn the enemy's left flank with Thackwell's and Valiant's columns, while Littler's column should assail the front.

The left column started half an hour before dawn of the 29th, and the two remaining columns at daybreak; and, notwithstanding the extreme intricacy of the ground, all three reached their appointed stations with remarkable precision. Littler's troops, under Gough's own directions, were the first to arrive, and halted about a mile from Maharajpur. Harry Smith had ridden through this village on the previous day; but it was now found that the enemy had advanced and entrenched it, occupying it both with infantry and artillery, which latter opened a desultory and harmless fire at extreme range. For an hour Gough, with a single staff officer, walked up and down within three hundred yards of the Mahratta sentries, making such observation as he could; but the plain was covered with high crops of corn which obstructed all view, and there was not so much as a mound to facilitate reconnaissance.

One thing, however, seemed to be clear. The Mahratta force in Maharajpur were beyond supporting distance of their main position at Chonda, which was a mile and a half in rear, and might therefore be isolated and overwhelmed. Gough sent for the four eight-inch howitzers, which were the only heavy pieces that he had been able to bring with him, and at half-past eight opened his attack upon Maharajpur.

Grant's troop of horse-artillery was the first to gallop to the front and engage the Mahratta guns on the left of the village. Alexander's troop joined him, and, though weight of metal was against them and the enemy's artillerymen showed both skill and resolution, the two advanced to within five hundred yards' range and silenced the hostile batteries, which were presently stormed by Valiant's brigade. Meanwhile Scott's cavalry had repulsed an advance of the Mahratta horse on the extreme left, and Littler's infantry, further to the right, was deploying within four hundred yards of the village under a heavy fire of round shot. The Fifty-Sixth Native Infantry wavered for a moment until urged forward by Gough himself, but the Thirty-Ninth never hesitated.

As the redcoats drew nearer the Mahratta artillery poured in a shower of grape and canister, and finally, as their ammunition failed, of horse-shoes and any scraps of iron that they could find, like the French at Fontenoy. Their gallant efforts were fruitless. The British made a final spring upon the guns, bayoneting the gunners, who stood nobly by their pieces to the last, and then engaged the Mahratta infantry in the rear. These too fought well; but by this time Valiant's success had made itself felt.

Within half an hour of the outset of the attack Maharajpur was in flames, every gun had been captured, and the force defending it had been practically destroyed. A few fugitives only, flying to their right instead of to their rear, took refuge in the village of Shirkapore, about a mile distant. It should seem that the Mahratta leaders had not only posted a detachment too far in front of their main position, but had repeated Tallard's blunder at Blenheim of occupying two villages too far apart to maintain a cross fire of artillery.

Thus the first stage of the fight had been successfully carried out, and that before the heavy howitzers had had time to come into action. It remained to deal with Shirkapore, which was strongly entrenched, and with the main position at Chonda. Little, it seems, could be seen of either, and, in fact, the Mahratta guns were so well concealed that even from the saddle only their muzzles could be perceived. However, Valiant was now directed to pass round Littler's rear, fall upon Shirkapore, and, having mastered it, to attack the Mahratta right of the main position, while Littler, supported by a regiment of light cavalry, should advance upon the front and Thackwell should manoeuvre round the Mahratta left to cut off their retreat. Once again the Mahratta gunners did their duty with desperate courage.

Valiant had to carry three entrenched positions one after another; and two successive commanding officers of the Fortieth fell wounded before the very muzzles of the guns before the batteries were captured. On the main position Grant again galloped to the front, and for more than half an hour engaged with his single troop a heavy battery of twelve cannon, which punished him severely. More than once he drove the enemy from their pieces, but, having no further support than a weak escort of cavalry, was unable to take advantage of his success or to prevent the Mahratta gunners from reopening fire.

However, Littler's infantry, headed by the Thirty-Ninth, carried all before them and rolled up the Mahratta line from its right to its left. The battle ended with the capture of a small work mounting four guns on the extreme Mahratta left, which was carried by the grenadiers of the Thirty-Ninth with a wing of the Fifty-Sixth Native Infantry in support. Thackwell's cavalry, being checked by an impassable ravine, was unable to pursue effectively; but the Mahrattas had been sufficiently well beaten, with the loss of fifty-six guns and of all their ammunition-waggons. As a fighting force they had ceased to exist.

Gough's casualties in this affair fell just short of eight hundred, almost exactly half of which number fell upon the Thirty-Ninth and Fortieth alone, the former counting two hundred and fourteen and the latter one hundred and sixty-two of all ranks killed and wounded. Reckoning the loss of the European artillery and of the British officers in native regiments, considerably less than one-half of the fallen were natives of India. The Sixteenth Bengal Grenadiers, with one hundred and seventy-nine casualties, alone bore their full share of the engagement, and behaved remarkably well; but the five remaining native battalions evidently contributed little to the work of the day. Indeed Harry Smith, who was present, says plainly that but for the Thirty-Ninth and Fortieth, the Mahratta resistance would not have been overcome—not, at any rate, as the battle was actually fought.

Details are so scanty, and our knowledge of the Mahratta position so imperfect, that it is difficult to form a judgement upon Gough's tactical handling of the action. It is, however, certain that the country immediately before the enemy's entrenchments was so blind that Gough was as much in the dark about them, until he came to close quarters, as was Napier at Miani and Hyderabad. In blaming Thackwell privately, for not obeying his orders and so failing to make effective pursuit, Gough mentions that between Maharajpur and the main position at Chonda there was a mile of open ground, with room enough for a brigade of cavalry to advance in line.

Harry Smith further records that the Mahratta batteries were most ably posted, each flanking and supporting the other by a heavy crossfire. By pushing his infantry into this cross-fire Gough obviously did exactly what the Mahrattas intended him to do. Harry Smith, in a private letter written at the time, declares that he earnestly advocated attack on the enemy's left flank, which would have immediately threatened their retreat. Whether, looking to the fact that Thackwell's cavalry was stopped short by an impassable ravine in this quarter, such an operation was feasible, is a question which cannot now be answered.

Possibly Gough would have considered it had he not, by his own confession, underrated his enemy. For this he blamed the "politicals," who gave him misleading intelligence; but, with the experience of Keane, Willoughby Cotton and Elphinstone before him, he might have been more cautious in accepting information from such a source.

In any case, whether rightly or wrongly, avoidably or unavoidably, he walked straight into the trap prepared for him. But it must be repeated that Napier had done exactly the same in Sind.

There remains the question as to the use of the various arms. Harry Smith, who was a friend of Gough, affirmed that they were not combined to such advantage as they might have been, but ascribed the defect, at any rate in some measure, to the inexperience and bad training of the officers of the Indian Army. There seems to be some ground for this criticism. In the first place, the heavy howitzers never came into action at all. The gunners complained that their pieces were brought up in line with the Thirty-Ninth (apparently after the first stage of the action) but were not allowed to move forward, as their officer desired, within eight hundred yards of the Mahratta position, at which range they could have knocked the Mahratta batteries to pieces, and rendered the advance of the infantry comparatively safe. On the other hand, Gough in private reproached this officer because he declined to open fire without orders; and then the question arises why the commander-in-chief, who had thrice summoned the howitzers, was not at hand to give him his orders. Whatever the explanation, these four heavy cannon were turned to no account whatever in the fight.

As to the field-batteries and horse-batteries, they seem to have galloped up at once to close quarters, and to have behaved with the greatest dash and intrepidity. The reason, a quite sufficient one, for their hastening forward was that they were outranged by the Mahratta guns and preferred, if they must be under fire, to open effective fire in return. But it should seem that they went into action too soon and too far ahead of the infantry. If the front of the Mahratta position were so blind that it could not be properly reconnoitred, the inference would seem to be that the attacking lines could have been moved up unobserved to within a comparatively short distance of the enemy's lines, that the artillery might then have been let loose, and that the rush of infantry could have followed directly that the Mahratta guns had been silenced. But to dogmatise upon these points, looking to the scantiness of our knowledge, would be certainly imprudent and probably unfair. (For the gunners' version of the action see Buckle's *Memoir of the Service of the Bengal Artillery*).

For the rest, Maharajpur set an extremely undesirable precedent for the presence of the governor-general, when not also commander-in-chief, with troops on active service in the field; and not only was

BATTLE OF MAHARAJPORE, Dec. 29, 1843.

Miles

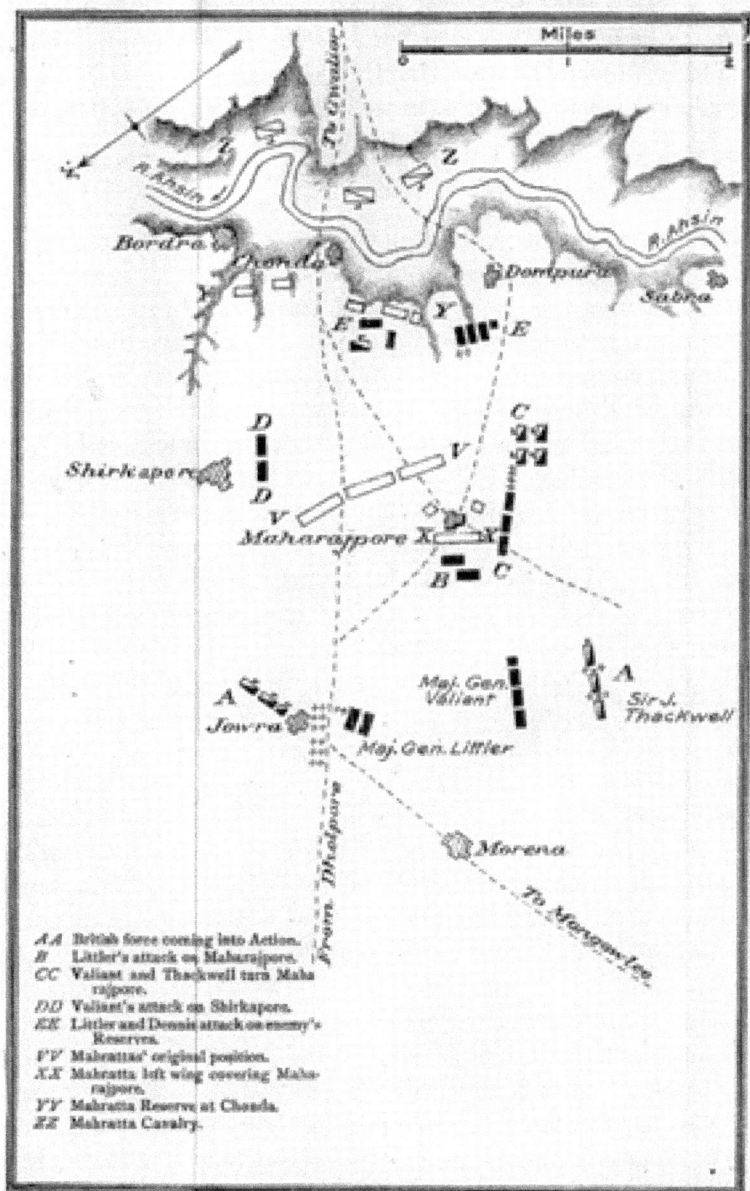

AA British force coming into Action.
B   Littler's attack on Maharajpore.
CC Valiant and Thackwell turn Maha-
    rajpore.
DD Valiant's attack on Shirkapore.
EE Littler and Dennis attack on enemy's
    Reserves.
VV Mahrattas' original position.
XX Mahratta left wing covering Maha-
    rajpore.
YY Mahratta Reserve at Chonda.
ZZ Mahratta Cavalry.

His Excellency there but sundry ladies also. Ellenborough showed real enjoyment at finding himself under fire; but Mrs. Harry Smith, who was an old campaigner, found (to use her husband's words) her command anything but satisfactory. Both governor-general and females had much better have stayed at home. When Lord Mornington proposed to accompany General Harris to Seringapatam in 1799, he was stopped by an abrupt sentence from his brother, Arthur Wellesley—

If I were in General Harris's situation and the Governor-general were to join the army, I should quit it.

These words might with advantage have been writ large on the walls of the governor-general's office at Calcutta.

On this same day Sir John Grey, pursuant to his orders, came up with his force to the Antri pass, and finding it, after reconnaissance, to be strongly occupied by the enemy, decided to turn it by the south and make for Panniar. His line of march, with all the encumbrances of an army in India, covered a length of about ten miles, and his route lay parallel to a range of hills, according to Grey some miles, but according to one of his brigadiers, who seems to be more accurate, only a few hundred yards to his right. In any case, 6 though he knew that he had left the Mahrattas in force somewhere on the other side of this range, Grey formed no flank-guard, nor even sent patrols of cavalry to the summit of these hills to watch them.

He was quite content with the orthodox vanguard and rearguard, and trailed away in the most casual fashion, till at about three in the afternoon he reached his halting-place, near Panniar, and the troops prepared to make themselves comfortable. Then suddenly there was a sound of guns in the rear of the column, still many miles distant, and native troopers came galloping into the lines in panic, crying out that the rearguard was attacked and was being cut to pieces. The assembly was sounded; the troops stood to arms; and reinforcements of cavalry, with a troop of horse-artillery, were hastily despatched to the help of the rearguard.

Then gradually it dawned upon Grey that the Mahrattas had been marching parallel with him all day, that their main body was in position on some high hills four miles to east of him, and that some of their guns, in a fortified village near Panniar, were firing at their leisure upon his huge column of baggage. His force included the British Buffs and Fiftieth, and five native battalions, organised in three brigades; a company of sappers and miners; with the Ninth Lancers and three

Death of Major General Churchill at Maharajpur

regiments of native horse, organised in two brigades. Of these he sent forward the Buffs and the sappers and miners alone over the crest of the hills, and, receiving from them a report that the Mahrattas were in great force on the other side, set the Fiftieth and two native regiments in motion to support them, under Colonel Anderson of the Fiftieth.

As these reached the foot of the ridge the Mahratta cannon-shot, fired from the other side, flew over them, and, when they deployed on the summit, the enemy's artillery fire redoubled, though the projectiles fell wide. Half a mile to his left Anderson could see the Buffs and a battery hotly engaged; while in his front was a deep rocky valley, filled with the enemy's infantry, and on the opposite side four guns in position. Anderson's brigade made its way to the foot of the valley under a heavy fire of grape and canister, and, taking shelter under a low bank, plied the enemy with musketry. The light was fast failing and Grey was nowhere to be found, so Anderson, taking matters into his own hands, cleared the valley and charged the guns. The Mahratta gunners stood firm to the last but were overwhelmed; and meanwhile the Buffs likewise had charged under a still heavier fire and captured eleven guns. The action came to an end at nightfall with the complete defeat of the Mahrattas.

Panniar is an affair even more obscure than Maharajpur. It is only certain that the Buffs bore the brunt of it and had seventy-two casualties, and that the Thirty-Ninth Native Infantry, which supported them, had sixty-two, and the Queen's Fiftieth forty-two. But out of a total loss of two hundred and thirteen killed and wounded, three European units claimed one hundred and sixteen, and eight native units ninety-seven, which figures tell their own story. The fight seems to have been a confused scrambling business to which General Grey had very little to say, the real work being done by Colonels Clunie of the Buffs and Anderson of the Fiftieth.

It was a matter of great good fortune that the commander of Anderson's brigade had disabled himself accidentally by a pistol shot a few days before the engagement, for he was quite unable to conduct even a peaceful brigade-field-day without coming to Anderson for preliminary instruction. Whether Grey himself was much more competent than this brigadier may be doubted. He declared the loss of the Mahrattas to be very heavy, which, in the circumstances, is most unlikely. It ought to have been very heavy, if Grey had used his cavalry aright, and had embraced the rare opportunity of attacking a Mahratta army on the march.

However, whatever the merits or demerits of the British commanders, the Gwalior campaign was successfully ended in one day. On the 31st the *rani* came into the British camp, and a treaty was signed whereby the *maharaja's* native army was reduced to ten thousand infantry and six thousand horse with thirty-two guns, and the native contingent of soldiers under British officers was raised to ten thousand. Thus was averted the formidable danger of a union between the trained forces of the Mahrattas and of the Sikhs against the British. Ellenborough, in order to make the most of the victory, distributed a bronze star for each of the two actions to all ranks; and then suddenly, in April 1844, he was recalled by the Court of Directors. He had not only signalised his tenure of office by a series of wars, but he had shown a marked preference for military men over civilians for every description of work in India. In fact he had carried reaction against Auckland's policy of trusting none but civilians to extreme lengths, having a partiality for soldiers that amounted to a passion. He said, in a farewell speech:

> The only regret I feel at leaving India is that of being separated from the army. The most agreeable, most interesting period of my life has been that which I have passed here in cantonments and camps.

Such an avowal was not likely to commend itself whether to Directors at home or to civil servants in India; being indeed so uncomplimentary as to be neither fair nor tactful to the latter. It is noteworthy that he received a long letter of sympathy from old Lord Wellesley, one of the greatest of governors-general, who confessed to him that he too had loved the army.

Curiously enough Ellenborough's predilection for things military has left a singular mark upon the army at large. He had given medals to all ranks for Jalalabad and the Afghan campaign, and bronze stars for Maharajpur and Panniar. There were only two precedents for such general rewards, the medal for Dunbar and the medal for Waterloo. There had long been discontent among those, below the rank of field-officer, who had fought through many campaigns in the Peninsula and elsewhere, but had missed Waterloo, because they had been left without any decoration; and in 1840, possibly on hearing of the medal for Ghazni, certain officers approached the Duke of Wellington on the subject. The duke replied that rewards were the sovereign's business, and that four hundred orders of different classes of the Bath had been granted to Peninsular officers over and above certain privileges of pay on promotion and of pay on retirement. The duke had spoken, and there was nothing more to be said.

Meanwhile the multiplication of medals not only for Indian campaigns but for the recent China campaign embittered the old grievance of the Peninsular officers, and in 1845 the Duke of Richmond presented a petition from them to the House of Lords on the subject. Wellington once again poured cold water on the movement, but had much ado to justify himself. He dismissed the Waterloo medal as an unprecedented reward for an unprecedented occasion, and the China medal as granted for an extraordinary expedition; but he was fain to admit that the queen had approved of Lord Ellenborough's medals, as it was necessary to mark the men's services. Then he stated the argument which, in his secret heart, weighed most heavily with him—it would be impossible to give a medal for the Peninsular War and to grant none for Egypt and Maida; and above all, medals could not be confined to the army but must be extended to the fleet. To all of this the Duke of Richmond answered, with sarcastic allusion to Ellenborough's Afghan medals:

Only suffer a disaster, and you will get a medal to revive your spirits.

It was evident that the matter could not end there. There was more severe fighting in India, shortly to be narrated; and in 1847 Sir de Lacy Evans again brought up the claim of Peninsular officers to medals in the Commons, when Lord John Russell announced that medals would be issued to all ranks who had been present at actions for which a medal had been issued to generals and field-officers. Clasps with the names of the various actions were added to the medals; the decoration was extended on the same principle to the navy; and since 1842 the grant of a medal, with or without clasps, to all ranks for every campaign has been recognised as a principle. The bronze star of Maharajpur and Panniar, made in that particular instance from captured cannon, has also been repeated for the march from Kabul to Kandahar in 1879 and for the earlier operations of the German war of 1914-1915, in each case—such is our poverty of invention—with a rainbow ribbon as in the case of the originals.

Our military medals are now so numerous that collections of them form a distinct branch of numismatics; and all this is due to Lord Ellenborough. Beyond all doubt his object was to strengthen the moral tone of a disheartened army; and there are many veteran officers, wearing countless ribbons on the left breast, who will smile grimly at the Duke of Richmond's comment. For the British Army has had its share of inglorious campaigns; and it is such that the British public delights specially to honour.

CHAPTER 3

The Sikhs Cross the Sutlej

Throughout this time and ever since the death of Ranjit Singh in 1839 there had been anarchy and chaos among the Sikhs in the Punjab. It would be lost labour to attempt to give an account of the intrigues, revolutions and assassinations that succeeded each other every few months. Actual power lay with the Praetorian Guard of the Punjab, the Khalsa or trained army, which, though organised and drilled according to European methods, was subject in time of peace to regimental committees, or *panchayats*, elected by the men; not in imitation of such remote models as the American levies of the War of Independence or the British volunteers of the War of the French Revolution and Empire, but in pursuance of the time-honoured practice of Indian village communities.

The great object of every successive ruler or puppet in the Punjab was to conciliate the favour of the army, which signified for one thing the regular payment of its wages; and since anarchy does not favour the steady collection of revenue, this was a constant difficulty. There was in fact no saying when the Khalsa might take power into its own hands; and then there was likely to be trouble. However closely the British agent at Lahore might watch events, it was impossible for him, or for any man, to forecast the future.

It was in September 1843 that events in the Punjab took a turn alarming to the government at Calcutta. Shere Sing, a reputed son of Ranjit, who for three years had ruled at Lahore and steadfastly followed his father's policy of friendship with the British, was murdered by his chief minister; and, after a few more murders a boy, Dhuleep Sing, was, with the help of the army, made nominally Maharaja, with one Hira Sing for chief minister. Forthwith his mother, the *rani*, her brother, Jewahir Sing, and her *paramour*, Lal Sing, became leaders, so to speak, of the opposition against Hira Sing; and both parties, as was natural, competed for the support of the army, by this time thoroughly hostile to the British.

Sir Hugh Gough saw the instant need for military precaution. On the south side of the Sutlej, for the safety of the Sikh states under British protection, the British held two dangerously isolated outposts, Ferozepore, an open cantonment actually on the bank of the river, and Ludhiana, a small fort nearly eighty miles to east of it. The nearest military station to these was Ambala, sixty-five miles from Ludhiana, and one hundred and fifty from Ferozepore; and the nearest station to Ambala was Meerut, one hundred and forty miles further to the south and east. On the other hand Lahore was within fifty miles, including the passage of the Sutlej, from Ferozepore, and the Sikh army was reckoned at any strength from forty thousand to one hundred thousand disciplined men, with at least two hundred guns.

Unwilling to provoke jealousy and suspicion in the Sikhs, Gough took advantage of some troops which were on their way to relieve those in Sind to reinforce Ferozepore, Ludhiana and Ambala; and presently he submitted a scheme for increasing the garrisons of the two former places to thirty-five thousand men apiece, with a cavalry brigade of two thousand to maintain communication between them; for raising the force at Ambala to six thousand men; and for placing the British regiments within easy reach on the hills to eastward. These arrangements were never fully carried out, Hira Sing proving himself after all to be shy of a quarrel with the British; but the forts both at Ferozepore and Ludhiana were strengthened, and orders were issued for the preparation of a pontoon-train for Ferozepore.

★★★★★★

So says Rait, *Life of Lord Gough*, i.; but the orders as to the pontoon may have been countermanded. At any rate the boats did not begin the journey up the Indus from Sukkur until July 1845. *I. O. S. C.*, vol. 4 of 1845, Proceedings of 4 July, Broadfoot to Gough, 16 June 1845.

★★★★★★

For the time, therefore, the alarm passed away. In July 1844, Sir Henry Hardinge arrived at Calcutta to succeed Ellenborough as Governor-General, and one of his first acts was to appoint George Broadfoot to be agent at Lahore, where he took up his duties on the 1st of November. Before he had been there three weeks the Sikh army, in Hardinge's words, sold Hira Sing for a rise in their wages; and he was

Lal Singh

hunted out and murdered, leaving the *Rani* for the moment supreme. This increase of the Sikh soldiers' pay raised it to double of that received by the Bengal *sepoys* of the British service, which, in itself, introduced a new element of anxiety.

A year earlier there had been a succession of mutinies among certain native regiments which had been ordered to embark for Sind. There seem to have been misunderstandings and blunders which might have been avoided by wiser handling; but there was also a very nasty spirit of insubordination underlying these mutinies, which spoke ill for the discipline of the Bengal native army. In fact, the native troops were already heading steadily towards the final catastrophe of 1857. Meanwhile it was only certain that the *sepoys* were afraid of the Sikhs, and that the Hindus among them were concealing their fright under the mask of religious scruples against fighting with them. There is no ground so holy as that which men stand in bodily fear of treading.

On the whole, therefore, the situation at the beginning of 1845 was one of decidedly greater peril; and Gough, even in August 1844, warned Hardinge that it would be only prudent to reinforce Ferozepore, Ludhiana and Ambala, and especially to post an European regiment at Ferozepore. He was under no illusions as to the formidable character of the Sikh army. He pointed out that the British had no field-artillery fit to cope with the heavy metal of the Sikhs, and that infantry alone must decide the fate of every battle in India. Hardinge, almost morbidly anxious not to give offence at Lahore, refused his permission, while admitting the force of Gough's arguments; and only upon Broadfoot's reports of renewed anarchy at Lahore after the death of Hira Sing, did he at last consent, in January 1845, to build additional barracks at Ferozepore for one European and two native battalions and for two troops of horse-artillery. Sir John Littler was appointed to the command of the place, and Gough took up his quarters at Ambala.

The months crept on with alternations of hope and fear; and Hardinge, while stealthily collecting troops, did his utmost to keep the peace. In June some Sikh cavalry crossed the south bank of the Sutlej, but Broadfoot readily accepted the explanation of the raid that was offered by the Lahore Durbar. In July the Sikhs, perturbed by announcements in the ever-mischievous Indian press, turned frantically to military preparations, and Broadfoot reported that by the winter the Sikh Army would be more efficient in material than it had been for years. But that army, he added, was now for the first time for many years dispersed, which was proof that hostilities were not immediately

Sikh Cavalry

contemplated.

At the end of the month Lal Sing, with a few followers, crossed the Sutlej, and Littler posted guards to prevent troops from crossing also; but Sept. nothing came of the incident. A few weeks later Broadfoot took exception to a change of tone in the communications of the Lahore Durbar, and was promptly censured by Hardinge, he wrote:

> It is the Governor-General's desire to show all forbearance and consideration to the young *Maharaja*, and on no account is the notorious immorality of his advisers to be made an occasion for breaking off the relations between the two governments ... if military operations should be forced upon us, the governor-general will have the satisfaction of knowing that every means of conciliation has been exhausted.

Broadfoot accepted the rebuke, but answered that the forbearance lately and still shown to the Sikhs was beyond all previous example, and had been carried to the point of danger.

This was in September; and in that month very perilous symptoms began to display themselves at Lahore. The army was slowly reassembling with scarcely concealed determination to change the government; and Sikh agents were abroad trying to corrupt the British *sepoys* and enlisting discharged men and deserters. Jawahir Sing, unable to pay the troops, saw no way out of his difficulties but a quarrel with the British, and said that he would send two brigades to Ferozepore to bring on a collision. On the 21st of September he was murdered, and on the 23rd the military committee or *panchayat* at Lahore assumed the government and at once made friendly overtures to Broadfoot; but on the very next day a brigade demanded to be led to Ferozepore. There were indeed two factions in the Khalsa, and no one could say which would prevail. Hardinge, on hearing all this, persisted in his confidence that the British frontier would not be violated, but he took all precautions and ordered up two more native battalions.

On the 6th of November the Lahore government sent Broadfoot the strongest assurances of friendship, which seemed to justify Hardinge. But the governor-general none the less equipped seven regiments of cavalry, eighteen battalions of infantry and eleven batteries of artillery with the means of moving at the shortest notice; and Gough directed reinforcements to be ready to march up from Meerut, though at Hardinge's request he presently cancelled the order. Broadfoot's intelligence was contradictory. On the 20th of November he reported that from forty to sixty thousand Sikhs would march at once to the Sutlej, and on the 23rd he announced that the project had been set aside.

Gough became very impatient of this vague information, but, when his staff attempted to obtain more exact details of the numbers and composition of the Sikhs, they were obstructed by the jealousy of the political agents. Keane, it will be remembered, had made the same complaint on his march to Kandahar, and had resolutely formed an intelligence-department of his own. It is curious to note how even good men and good soldiers such as George Broadfoot and Henry Lawrence allowed their heads to be turned by their own importance when acting as political agents.

★★★★★★

For the preceding paragraphs see Rait, *Life of Lord Gough,* i. 378-387; Broadfoot's *Career of Major George Broadfoot; India Office Secret Consultations,* Vol. IV. of 1845, Proceedings of 15 Aug.; Broadfoot to Dhuleep Sing, 28 June; to Indian govt., 14 July; Vol. V. of 1845, Proceedings of 5 Sept.; Indian govt, to Broadfoot, 5 Sept.; Littler to Gough, 5 Sept.; Vol. VI. of 1845, Proceedings of 6 Dec; Broadfoot to Indian govt., 15, 16 Sept., 6 Nov.; to Gough and Capt. P. Nicolson, 10 Sept.; Indian govt, to Broadfoot, 2 Oct.; Hardinge to Gough, 24 Nov. 1845.

★★★★★★

By the end of November Littler at Ferozepore became anxious, and asked for an additional European regiment. Gough supported the request, which reached Hardinge at Ambala on the 3rd of December; but the governor-general, while sanctioning the movement, delayed the issue of actual orders until the 7th; and by that time it was too late. On the 8th Broadfoot gave definite information that the Sikhs would cross the Sutlej immediately; and the governor-general, at considerable personal risk, rode to Ludhiana, and on his own responsibility ordered all but the weaker men of the garrison to be withdrawn to Bassian, some twenty-five miles to the south-west, where lay the principal grain depot of the army.

On the 11th the Sikhs began the passage of the Sutlej, and on that same day Gough ordered his cavalry to advance from Ambala, following himself with the infantry on the 12th. The situation was not too comfortable, Hardinge's extreme reluctance to give any pretext for hostilities having moved him to take great risks. In all he had gathered together on the frontier some thirty thousand men; but they were

SIKH SOLDIERS.—(FROM A SKETCH BY AN OFFICER OF THE BENGAL ENGINEERS.)

widely dispersed. Littler at Ferozepore had about seven thousand, with which he was confident of holding his own; but the nearest troops to him were the five thousand men at Ludhiana, now mostly on march to Bassian, which itself was sixty miles from Ferozepore; the nearest force to Bassian was ten thousand men at Ambala, eighty miles away; and the remaining eight or nine thousand lay at Meerut nearly one hundred and twenty miles from Ambala. (See list following).

★★★★★★

Ferozepore: H.M. 62nd; 12th, 14th, 27th, 33rd, 44th, 54th, 63rd N.I.; 8th N.L.C., 3rd N. Irreg. Horse, 2 horse and 2 field-batteries.

Ludhiana: H.M. 50th; 11th, 26th, 42nd, 48th, 73rd N.I.; detacht. N. Cav.; 2 horse-batteries.

Ambala: H.M. 9th, 31st, 80th; 16th, 24th, 41st, 45th, 47th N.I.; H.M. 3rd L.D.; 4th, 5th N.C.; artillery; H.M. 29th at Kasauli; 1st Bengal Eur. Regt. (102nd) at Sabathu.

Meerut: H.M. 10th Foot; 5 (?) battalions N.L; H.M. 9th and 16th Lancers; 3rd N.L.C.; artillery with 26 guns.

★★★★★★

The troops had, at any rate for the most part, not been brigaded and knew little of their comrades or commanders; and transport was scanty and unorganised. This last was no fault of Gough. He had wished to make timely provision but had been checked by Hardinge, who likewise acted upon the best of his judgement, for political reasons. By Hardinge's urgent request Broadfoot arranged for supply-depots for ten thousand men at intervals of twenty miles between Meerut and Ferozepore, and got the work accomplished within five days, though only by great exertion and high-handed methods, (*Career of George Broadfoot*). All of these troubles may well have been unavoidable, but they did not give a very fair chance to the commander-in-chief.

The only thing to be done was to hustle the different detachments together as rapidly as possible, and hurry them forward toward the isolated post at Ferozepore. On the 16th the Ludhiana force and the cavalry from Ambala united at Badhni, thirteen miles west of Bassian, and on the 17th the rest of the men from Ambala joined them a short march further to westward. The force was now organised into one cavalry division under General Thackwell and three infantry divisions under Generals Harry Smith, Gilbert and McCaskill, but of these one only of the infantry divisions was complete, the other two being practically no more than brigades. (See list following).

52

Cavalry Division: Thackwell.

Mactier's Brigade:	9th Irreg. Horse, ½ 4th L.C.
Gough's „	5th L.C, Gov.-genl.'s Bodyguard
White's „	H.M. 3rd L.D., ½ 4th L.C.

1st Infantry Division: Smith.

1st Brigade: (Bolton)	H.M. 31st, 24th and 47th N.I.
2nd „ (Wheeler)	H.M. 50th, 42nd, 48th N.I.

2nd Infantry Division: Gilbert.

3rd Brigade:	45th N.I., 2nd Grenadiers N.I.
4th „	16th Grenadiers N.I.

3rd Infantry Division: McCaskill.

5th Brigade:	H.M. 9th, 26th and 73rd N.I.
6th „	Nil.

The entire body counted five regiments of cavalry, five troops of horse-artillery and two field-batteries with forty-two guns, and thirteen battalions, of which four only were British. Its strength may be reckoned at between eleven and twelve thousand men.

So far the men had travelled rather more than one hundred miles in five days, and there had been only one trifling affair with the enemy at Badhni. The next stage was to the village of Mudki, and on the morning of the 18th Gough, with all due precaution, covered his advance with a party of irregular horse which was accompanied by Broadfoot. The Sikhs likewise had sent mounted parties forward; and on reaching Mudki Broadfoot found the village in the occupation of the enemy, and sent his report back to Gough, who was three miles in rear.

Thereupon Gough changed his formation from column of route to order of battle and marched on. On reaching Mudki he found that the Sikhs had withdrawn from it, and accordingly he halted and occupied the place. The men were utterly exhausted and suffering grievously from thirst. It is recorded that at the penultimate halt, two miles from Mudki, there were scarcely fifty men of the Thirty-First with the colours, while the stragglers were scattered for miles in rear.

Gradually they dragged themselves up. Between two and three o'clock the camels began to come in; and the weary and hungry troops bestirred themselves to cook their food. Whether or not the Sikhs were shrewd enough to think this a good moment for attack

BATTLE OF MUDKI

must be a matter of conjecture; but certain it is that Broadfoot, while lunching with Hardinge, received messages from his cavalry and his intelligencers that the enemy was advancing. He rode out instantly to confirm the report with his own eyes, and, returning, pointed to a great cloud of dust with the words:

There, Your Excellency, is the Sikh army.

There was and is no certain information of the enemy's strength, but the lowest estimate states it as eight to ten thousand horse, two to three thousand foot, and about twenty-two guns. It is possible that their infantry were more numerous; but Gough's own estimate of fifteen to twenty thousand foot and forty guns seems certainly to be excessive. The ground for a mile in front of the British was open ploughed fields, beyond which came a deep belt of dense jungle and stunted trees. The Sikhs were still from two to three miles distant when the alarm was first given, and there was plenty of time to make dispositions for receiving the attack in the open; but Gough, perhaps fearful lest his enemy should escape him, hurried his cavalry and horse-artillery forward, and the Sikhs, observing their approach, halted in the jungle.

They then opened fire from their cannon, and the British horse-batteries, galloping up to the edge of the jungle, unlimbered and answered them, though they could see little to guide their aim but the smoke of the enemy's guns. This duel lasted about half-an-hour, when the two field-batteries came up to join their five brethren of the horse; while Gough's and White's brigades trotted forward to protect their right, and Mactier's brigade to cover their left flank. The exchange of cannon-shot was then renewed, when, after about another half-hour, the enemy's fire slackened, their guns having been either silenced for the time or withdrawn.

At the same time great masses of Sikh horse advanced as if to attempt a great enveloping movement. Four horse-batteries, two on each flank, were thereupon pushed into the jungle to foil them. The British cavalry by brilliant charges quickly made an end of the menace; and the batteries were then ordered once more to close to the centre in order to support the advance of the infantry.

The line had meanwhile been formed, with Wheeler's brigade of Smith's division on the right, and then, in succession to the left of it, Bolton's brigade, the four battalions of McCaskill's division and the three battalions of Gilbert's.

★★★★★★

Gough says that he had but twelve battalions in action, from which I infer that the 24th N.I. was left in Mudki as baggage guard. The places of the twelve battalions can only be filled by conjecture, though it is certain that the 50th was on the extreme right. I take their order to have been as follows:

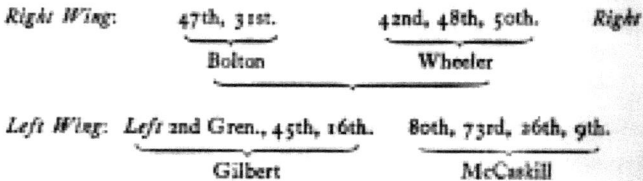

Right Wing:	47th, 31st.	42nd, 48th, 50th.	*Right*
	Bolton	Wheeler	

Left Wing:	*Left* 2nd Gren., 45th, 16th.	80th, 73rd, 26th, 9th.
	Gilbert	McCaskill

★★★★★★

By this time it was almost dusk of a short winter's day, and the dust was so thick that little could be seen. The batteries tried to struggle forward, but the jungle grew steadily denser as they advanced, and only with great difficulty could the guns force their way through it. Close in their front the enemy stood firm, both artillery and infantry; and the British gunners and horses began to fall fast under a destructive blast of grape and musketry. The infantry went forward with difficulty, the jungle forbidding any steady regularity of line, and the enemy's sharpshooters, hidden in trees, picked off man after man with galling and demoralising accuracy.

The *sepoys*, all inwardly fearful of the Sikhs, began to hang back. Wheeler's brigade, threatened at the outset by Sikh cavalry, had formed square, but only the Fiftieth obeyed Smith's order to re-form line and advance, the two native battalions remaining in square and firing in all directions, even on the rear of the Fiftieth. Harry Smith decided the combat here by riding into the thick of the enemy's infantry with one of the Fiftieth's colours, when his white soldiers speedily dispersed them with the bayonet and mastered the guns.

Immediately on his left Bolton's brigade was similarly tried. Bolton himself, adjuring the Thirty-First to be steady and fire low, was mortally stricken. Colonel Byrne, who commanded the regiment, also fell severely wounded, but his men stormed forward, shattered the Sikh infantry with their fire and carried their batteries with the bayonet. Still further to the left McCaskill's and Gilbert's battalions were less severely engaged; but everywhere there was sharp fighting, and Hardinge, who had lent most of his staff to Gough, was in the thick of

3RD LIGHT DRAGOONS

it. Between dusk and darkness the confusion was very great, and the British troops undoubtedly fired into each other. Sir Frederick Currie, the Secretary to the Indian Government, wrote that twice he and the governor-general were under heavy and destructive fire from British guns and musketry, and that, in the opinion of both, half of the casualties at Mudki were caused by friends.

The Sikh Army was not less bewildered than the British. It should seem that their infantry, when first driven back by Wheeler's brigade, retired blindly to a flank, passed across the greater part of the British line in column, and was then hustled back once more across the front of Wheeler. Altogether Mudki was a blind affair from first to last, and was finally stopped by darkness.

Gough's casualties amounted to eight hundred and seventy-two, of which number five hundred and six were Europeans, and three hundred and sixty-six were natives of India. The senior officers suffered heavily. Of Gough's staff Sir Robert Sale, quarter-master-general, and two more were killed, and Major Patrick Grant and two more were wounded, Grant himself dangerously. Among the divisional leaders McCaskill was killed, and of the Brigade-Commanders Bolton and Wheeler were wounded, the former mortally.

The Third Light Dragoons lost two officers, fifty-six men and over one hundred horses killed, and thirty-five of all ranks wounded—the result of charging against batteries. The Thirty-First had one hundred and fifty-seven casualties; and the Fiftieth one hundred and nine, the Ninth fifty-two, and the Eightieth twenty-four. Of the native regiments the Forty-Second Native Infantry had eighty-nine killed and wounded and the Second Grenadiers seventy-one. The Forty-Seventh, which was brigaded with the Thirty-First, counted not one-tenth of its casualties. The significance of these figures is not to be mistaken. The brunt of the work fell upon the British, and the *sepoys* did not do their fair share of the work.

The enemy's losses were presumed to be severe and they left seventeen guns in the hands of the victors; but, taken as a whole, the action seems to have been unsatisfactory and unduly costly. Harry Smith is the critic who deplored the advance into the jungle instead of awaiting the Sikhs on the plain; and, though all of his comments upon this campaign should be received with caution, it is not obvious why Gough should have hurried his troops headlong into woodland fighting in their first action. Men, unless they be veterans of experience, invariably shoot each other on these occasions; and these soldiers knew

BATTLE OF MOODKEE, December 18, 1845.

Miles

H

H

H

H

Sikh Cav'y

Sikh Cav'y

Sikh Cav'y

G

Sikh Infantry and Guns

G

G

B A

C

D

F E

Order of Encampment

G G'g Camp

C in C'g Camp

MOODKEE

REFERENCES.

A Brig. M. White.
B Brig. J. B. Gough.
C Brig. W. Mactier.
D Maj.-Gen. Sir H. Smith.
E Maj.-Gen. W. R. Gilbert.
F Maj.-Gen. Sir John McCaskill.
G The British Cavalry turning the
    enemy's flanks.
H The Sikh Army in full flight.

neither their commanders nor their comrades outside their own regiments, and were further exhausted by a succession of forced marches. It is, therefore, hardly surprising that the *sepoys* hung back and fired upon those who went forward. On the other hand, Gough may have apprehended that the Sikhs would decline an action if they found him ready; and his instinct to fly at an oriental enemy as soon as they showed themselves was not, in principle, unsound.

The troops were too much fatigued to follow up their success, though Gough himself did not leave the field until two o'clock in the morning; and the 19th was devoted to rest and to care of the wounded. In the evening the Twenty-Ninth Foot, the Hundred and Second and two native regiments, came up, together with a couple of eight-inch howitzers, the only heavy pieces with the army. Their arrival enabled the skeleton brigades of the divisions commanded by Gilbert and by Wallace (who had succeeded McCaskill) to be filled out somewhat, though not without fresh dislocations, (see list following); and meanwhile Colonels Hicks and Ryan took the places of Bolton and Wheeler as brigadiers in Harry Smith's division.

★★★★★★

2nd Division: Gilbert.
> 3rd Brigade: (Taylor) H.M. 29th; 45th N.I.
> 4th   „   (Maclaran) 102nd Foot; 2nd and
> 16th Grenadiers N.I.

3rd Division: Wallace.
> 5th Brigade: H.M. 9th; 26th and 73rd N.I.
> 6th   „   H.M. 80th.

★★★★★★

Finally Hardinge, who was junior to Gough in the army, waived his rank as Governor-General and volunteered to serve as his second in command. Since he would not, as a soldier, see a battle go forward without taking part in it, possibly it was better that some definite function should be assigned to him. At Mudki he had, so to speak, made himself generally useful, apparently taking charge of the Third Division after McCaskill's fall, (so I judge from Hardinge's *Life of Lord Hardinge).* From henceforward he commanded the left wing.

Gough's first objective was still Ferozepore, and his first purpose a junction with Littler's detachment which lay there. But, if his force was divided, so also was that of the Sikhs; one portion of their army, under Tej Sing, being employed in watching Littler, while the other, under Lal Sing, lay in a strongly entrenched position at Ferozeshah,

60

from eight to nine miles northwest of Mudki, barring one direct road from that place to Ferozepore and flanking another, which ran parallel to it from one to two miles further to the south. On the 20th Gough sent orders to Littler to leave a small guard only to hold his cantonments, and to slip away with the bulk of his troops to join him. Where the junction was to be effected does not appear, though presumably some definite place was fixed; but it is certain that Littler was instructed to move to south of the Sikh entrenchments at Ferozeshah. These orders reached Littler safely on the evening of the 20th, and at about the same time Gough summoned his generals to him to explain to them his plan of attack for the morrow.

At this point we strike against a mystery which has never been cleared up, namely the quarter from which Gough originally designed to assail the Sikh position. All information went to show that it was, roughly speaking, quadrilateral, (more accurately it was oval; but it is simpler to treat it as quadrilateral for purposes of description), in shape, measuring roughly speaking about a mile and a half from north to south, and nearly a mile from east to west. Of the four sides the northern, southern and western were reported to be strongly entrenched and surmounted by guns of very heavy metal, (*Broadfoot*). The approach to these three faces was further encumbered by belts of jungle. The eastern face on the contrary, namely that which looked towards Mudki, was unprotected and looked out upon perfectly open country. Obviously, therefore, if Gough desired no more than the capture of the position and the opening of the road to Ferozepore, this eastern side offered most advantages for an attack.

But if, as his instructions to Littler seem to suggest, he desired not only to drive Lal Sing away but to intercept his retreat upon Tej Sing's army and upon Lahore, uniting first with Littler's detachment for that purpose, then plainly the southern face was preferable. It is, of course, possible that Gough designed to assail the eastern face himself, and leave to Littler the task of striking at the flank of the flying enemy from the south; but it does not appear that Littler received from him any orders except to move out and effect a junction with Gough to south of Ferozeshah. This would mean a march of some nine miles, with no further obstruction—provided of course that Tej Sing's vigilance could be eluded—than the passage of a broad dry water-course. Two things only are certain in respect of Gough's conference with his generals on the morning of the 20th, first, that Hardinge was not present, his Military Secretary taking his place, and secondly, that on the morrow the generals either required fresh instructions or received no instructions at all respecting their place and mode of attack.

★★★★★★

Harry Smith, *Autobiography*, ii., says, "Nor were generals of division made the least aware of how or what or where they were to attack." Though, as I have said, I receive Harry Smith's comments on this campaign with caution, he, being a divisional general, should speak with some authority. Still, other generals may have received more precise orders than himself.

★★★★★★

In any case Gough's army marched at 4 a.m. on the 21st, leaving two native regiments at Mudki for the protection of the wounded and the baggage. Moving in column of route through pitch darkness it made very slow progress, and, apparently, took the best part of seven hours to traverse four or five miles and to deploy within about two miles of the eastern face of the Sikh entrenchments. At 10.30 there was a halt, when the men breakfasted off the contents of their haversacks; and half-an-hour later all was ready. Gough, who had apparently ridden forward to see what he could for himself, returned to Hardinge, who was eating with his staff, and said, "Sir Henry, if we attack at once, I promise you a splendid victory."

Hardinge, much surprised, beckoned Gough to follow him to a clump of trees fifty yards away; and there Gough repeated his suggestion for an immediate attack. Hardinge insisted that the junction with Littler must first be effected, which signified the movement of the army southward to meet him. Gough pleaded that such a manoeuvre would mean the abandonment of his communications with Ambala and of his wounded at Mudki. Hardinge would not yield; and it is not difficult to supply his arguments by imagination. Gough, on his side, was not less resolute, urging in particular that this was the shortest day in the year and that time was all important. Finally Hardinge closed the discussion with the words:

Then, Sir Hugh, I must exercise my civil powers as Governor-general and forbid the attack until Littler has come up.

★★★★★★

It is quite impossible to reconcile all the conflicting narratives of this apparently simple matter. Mr. Rait's account, based on Gough's, is itself full of contradictions. He says (ii.) that Gough's force after covering four miles found itself face to face with the right of the Sikh entrenchments. As the Sikh front may be assumed to be facing eastward, towards Mudki, the Sikh right would be the south. Again he says that the words "Right wheel into line," if given at 11 a m. would have brought on an action; and that at this same hour the army was fronting the eastern face of the Sikh position. Now if an army were in open column, facing westward, the words "Right wheel into line" would change its front to the north. This would be correct for an attack on the south front of the entrenchments; but for an attack on the east front absurd. Hardinge (*Life of Lord Hardinge*) says that a circuitous route was taken, but implies that, after Sir Henry Hardinge gave his decision that Littler's arrival must be awaited, Gough's troops simply sat still—in other words that Gough had already brought them over against the southern front.

On the other hand, Gough's despatch says that, after debouching four miles on the road to Ferozeshah, his force, instead of advancing to the direct attack (that is to say upon the eastern face) of the enemy's works manoeuvred to their (the Sikhs') right, that is to say, to attack the southern face; and Harry Smith confirms this by saying (ii.) that Gough's force almost crossed the front of the enemy's position. It must be added that Gough's despatch is confused and inaccurate. He says that the longest sides of the enemy's quadrilateral were those facing Ferozepore (westward) and the "open country"—a vague term, which, however, can only be construed as eastward. The shorter sides he describes as looking towards the Sutlej—a vague term which might mean either westward or northward—and Mudki, which can only mean eastward. He then says that he attacked the face towards "the open country," *i.e.* the western face, and this curiously enough is confirmed by the very minute account of the action in Innes's *History of the Bengal European Regiment*.

★★★★★★

The governor-general had spoken, and Gough was bound to obey. The army was set in motion again in a south-westerly direction, and before long a cloud of dust to westward announced the approach of Littler. It was past noon before that officer himself rode up, ahead of his troops, and a full hour later before his two regiments of horse, six battalions and twenty-one guns, marched in to the village of Misriwala, upon the left of Gough's array.

★★★★★★

Littler's Force:

    7th Brigade: (Reid) H.M. 62nd; 12th and 14th N.I.

    8th   ,,   (Ashburnham) 33rd, 44th, 54th N.I.

    Cavalry Brigade: (Harriott) 8th N.L.C.; 3rd Irreg. N.C.

    Artillery. 21 guns.

★★★★★★

Littler seems to have slipped away from Tej Sing's front deftly enough, thanks to the old trick of leaving his camp standing, and there was no sign that the Sikh leader was following him. But he had not started until 8 a.m., which seems to indicate that, if Gough had from the first determined to attack at 11 a.m., he did not count upon Littler to take any serious part in the fight.

Gough's force was now some eighteen thousand strong, with two heavy howitzers and sixty-three pieces of light and heavy artillery; and he made immediate preparations for attack upon the south front of the Sikh entrenchments. On the extreme right was a troop of horse-artillery, and then, in succession to the left, Taylors and Maclaran's brigades of Gilbert's division. In the centre were massed three troops of horse-artillery, two field-batteries, the heavy howitzers and some rockets. On the left of these stood Wallace's division, no more than four battalions, then another horse-battery, then Littler's division, and on the extreme left Littler's cannon, one and a half batteries of field-guns, and two troops of horse-artillery. In second line Harry Smith's division formed the reserve, its two brigades being stationed on either flank of the massed guns, Ryan's on the right and Hicks's to the left. Littler's cavalry, being left at his own disposal, took post to his left rear; and the rest of the horse was aligned on the reserve in support of each wing.

The Sikh position seems to have followed the conformation of a cluster of low hillocks, which rose about ten feet above the plain, and encircled the village of Ferozeshah. It was, as has been said, roughly a quadrilateral, and the comment of one who took part in the fight that "this bull was all horns" implies that no one point in it, despite of the reports of spies, was much weaker than another. The fortifications, however, were not unusually formidable, having neither deep ditches nor high ramparts; in fact they were simply good shelter-trenches. But within them were nearly one hundred guns, one-quarter of them of really heavy metal and most of them of greater calibre than any of Gough's pieces, except his two heavy howitzers.

Moreover, even those of equal calibre with Gough's were far

weightier in metal, could fire a greater charge of powder and were therefore effective at a longer range. The Sikh artillery-men, further, worshipped their guns, and could be trusted to work them with skill and to stand by them to the end. Lastly, they were backed by a strong force of good foot. It was morally certain that the brunt of the work in storming such a position must fall upon the infantry.

The marshalling of the troops into array took up much valuable time. It was 3.30 p.m. before the action began, and even then the first attack seems to have been launched prematurely. Littler upon the extreme left opened it with an advance of his artillery, which hurried on rapidly within range of grape-shot and for a time drove the gunners of the opposing batteries from their guns. His two brigades then advanced, Reed's leading with Ashburnham's in support, in such order as they could preserve while pushing through the belt of jungle, and on emerging into the open, within three hundred yards of the entrenchments, were met by a terrific blast of grape.

Reed gave the order to charge, and the Sixty-Second rushed on halfway over the open space towards the guns. Two hundred and sixty of them were mowed down in ten minutes, but success was within their grasp when they wavered and hesitated. Their officers made frantic efforts to urge them forward, but in vain. They gave way and went back; and the two *sepoy* battalions that were brigaded with them, though they had not suffered a third of their losses, went back with them, if they had not gone before them. Ashburnham's brigade seems to have made little effort to advance, and the whole division drew back out of range and remained out of action for the rest of the day.

Meanwhile Gough, observing Littler's advance and fearful lest he should gain the trenches unsupported, hurried Wallace's and Gilbert's divisions to the attack. Their progress through the jungle was difficult, for the Sikh shot cut down heavy branches and trees in all directions, making the preservation of order almost impossible. They emerged into a dense bank of dust and smoke. The British line far overlapped the southern face of the entrenchments, and the men, eager to close but seeing only a comparatively short row of flashes before them, crowded in towards the centre. Thus they masked the fire of the British batteries, the greater number of which had already pressed forward beyond the jungle as the only chance to avoid being blown out of the field. The left of Wallace's division seems to have given way; but the right, or at any rate the Ninth Foot, stormed forward, as did also the British battalions of Gilbert's division.

Even Gilbert's right brigade staggered for a moment under the tempest of Sikh shot, but Hicks's brigade, coming up from the reserve, melted into one line with it and carried it onward. The edge of the ditch before the Sikh trenches was strewn, with stumps and branches of trees through which the men struggled, blaspheming hideously; and then, falling upon the Sikh gunners with the bayonet, they made an end of them. Quickly re-forming upon the low heights they plunged down among the Sikh infantry in rear of the guns and drove them back into their camp. So dense were the smoke and dust that the darkness was as the darkness of night.

Meanwhile on the left Harry Smith, observing the order of Littler's attack, had predicted its failure to Hardinge, who had directed Smith to bring up his division without delay. Smith had only one brigade, Ryan's, under his hand, but he set it in motion at once, and arrived just in time to check a counter-attack by the Sikhs upon the gap opened by the retreat of Littler's division and of Wallace's left. His advance was a difficult matter, his progress being encumbered by a crowd of broken troops, though some of the Fourteenth Native Infantry of Reed's brigade rallied upon him and went forward with him. To meet the Sikh counter-attack he was obliged to wheel up the right of his brigade, but his whole dependence was upon the Fiftieth, which bore down all opposition with the bayonet, and, rushing on, captured the batteries opposed to them.

Thus the British had obtained a footing from end to end of the southern face; and just at this time, as it seems, the Third Light Dragoons, being ordered to attack a battery on the eastern face, charged headlong over the entrenchments, cut down the Sikh gunners, and then swept with loud shouts over tent-pegs, tent-ropes, guns and every description of obstacle straight through the Sikh reserves to the opposite side of the enemy's position, where they rallied, having lost half their number, a mere handful of unconquerable men.

Meanwhile the Hundred and Second had joined the Ninth, and, bearing to the left, were attacking in flank the batteries on the western front of the position, capturing and spiking gun after gun. They then turned to traverse the central street of the Sikh camp towards Ferozeshah, when the explosion of a magazine in the middle of them destroyed many and scattered the Hundred and Second in all directions. Those that had passed the magazine bore away to their right, those in rear of it to their left, where they joined Harry Smith, who, having re-formed the Fiftieth, was pressing on upon the village. Here there was a stiff fight and heavy slaughter of the Sikhs, but the buildings were carried. More and more men of Gilbert's and Wallace's divisions joined Harry Smith, and, still advancing, he pushed on through the enemy's camp for half-a-mile beyond the village, when darkness brought him to a standstill.

The confusion by this time was unspeakable. The Sikh camp had caught fire in many places; tents were blazing up fiercely for a few minutes and then dying down; magazines, great and small, were exploding with savage flashes; but no light could pierce through the blinding fog of dust and smoke. Hardinge, dreading lest the men should fire upon each other, and finding his progress barred by the burning camp, collected all that he could and made them lie down on the camp's skirts, so as to shelter them as far as possible from the Sikh batteries which were still firing from the north and east. Harry Smith, north of the village, found himself with some three thousand men of various regiments round him, all so mad with excitement as to be almost unmanageable. He listened and looked eagerly, though in vain, for Gilbert to come up on his right; and at last realising that he was isolated and alone, he drew up his troops in a semi-circle, with his right flank towards the village.

Hardly was the manoeuvre completed, when the Sikhs attacked his right, where the *sepoys* gave way at once. With some difficulty he contracted his formation, in time to face the enemy, who now closed upon him from all sides with cannon, swivel-guns and musketry, firing and shouting and beating the French *pas de charge* on their drums. Finally they brought up a gun to his rear, from which they poured in a continual fire of grape. The native troops became more and more excited and unsteady, but the British soldiers, despite of heavy losses, stood firm; and after waiting thus till two or three o'clock in the morning, Harry Smith made a feint of a counter-attack, and under cover of the noise and smoke filed round the western side of Ferozeshah. Continuing his course southward he came first upon the wounded men of the Sixty-Second, who had fallen in Littler's abortive attack, and further on to the village of Misriwala, where, finding some formed artillery and cavalry and a mob of some thousands of stragglers and lost men, he came for the time to a halt.

Throughout this time Hardinge and Gough were keeping their men together as best they could. When they met, apparently early in the evening, they agreed that the situation was most critical, but neither for a moment dreamed of any other course but to stand firm and fight the battle out. There were many whose hearts failed them and gave weaker counsels. Messages were brought to Smith that the governor-general advised retreat upon Ferozepore. He declined to believe it and he was right, for the two chiefs never wavered for a moment. Towards midnight the fire of a heavy Sikh gun became so galling that Hardinge called upon the Eightieth and Hundred and Second to silence it. They advanced in two lines at the double, exchanged a volley or two with the Sikh infantry round the gun, which belched out double charges of grape to the last, and then with a rush they fell upon the enemy, captured not only the gun which was the principal offender, but a battery of lighter pieces, spiked them and returned, many fewer than had started, but with their duty done. In fact the spirit of the British troops was not in the least impaired.

They were utterly exhausted after twenty-four hours on foot with very little food; they were suffering terribly from thirst, for the Sikhs kept sharp-shooters round the wells and shot down all who approached them; and the night was bitterly and cruelly cold. Yet Hardinge, visiting in succession the Ninth, Twenty-Ninth, Thirty-First and Fiftieth, old comrades of the Peninsula, found one and all in good heart, worthy of such dauntless leaders as himself and Gough.

To the great relief of both Harry Smith joined them shortly before dawn. Smith at Misriwala had been met by a staff-officer who, evidently quite unnerved and for the time insane, ordered him to collect every man and march for Ferozepore. Refusing point blank to obey, Smith found an officer who could guide him to Gough; and so once again the army was more or less re-united. Hardinge, during the dark hours, secretly sent Napoleon's sword—a present from Wellington—to safe keeping; ordered all State papers at Mudki to be destroyed; and insisted on the withdrawal of Prince Waldemar of Prussia, who had accompanied the army as an amateur, to a place of safety. The night was the most anxious ever spent by a governor-general and a commander-in-chief in India; but slowly and painfully it passed away, and at dawn both were cheerful and confident.

The morning broke with a dense mist, but when this had been dispelled by the sun, it was seen that the Sikhs had re-occupied the entrenchments captured and abandoned by the British on the preceding day. Three troops of horse-artillery at once galloped forward to open upon them, and were answered by some heavy pieces which blew up two or three ammunition waggons. But the Sikh fire soon grew feeble; the infantry advanced with a shout and swept over the trenches and through the camp, meeting with little or no resistance, to the northern face, where they halted, as if on parade, while Gough and Hardinge rode down the line amid wild cheering. The position had been taken at last, and over seventy guns with it, while most of Lal Sing's infantry had evidently retreated during the night.

A certain proportion of men were ordered to fall out, some to fetch water and others to see to the captured guns, when the cavalry, which had been sent forward to watch the retiring enemy, sent in reports that they had been checked by a second Sikh force, advancing from the direction of Ferozepore. This was the army of Tej Sing which, having discovered the withdrawal of Littler, was following him up. For a moment even Gough was inwardly, though not outwardly, dismayed. His men and horses were exhausted, and his artillery-ammunition was almost spent; and here was a fresh enemy in superior numbers before him, and a fresh battle to be fought. He disposed his force in a hollow square round the village of Ferozeshah, Gilbert's division in the centre facing west, and the two remaining divisions facing north and south, following, in fact, the line of the Sikh entrenchments.

The seven troops of horse-artillery moved to the front and opened fire, but were soon obliged to retire by weight of superior metal and by lack of ammunition. The guns were then mostly placed in prolongation of the northern face, though three were posted at the north-eastern angle; and for these last some forty or fifty rounds were collected from the Sikh ammunition captured on the previous day. Tej Sing now opened a heavy and destructive cannonade upon Gough's infantry, and Gough was fain to endure it, for his men were too weary to attack with the bayonet and had hardly a cartridge in pouch. Had the Sikh leader known it, he had only to continue the fire from his heavy guns to win an easy victory, for even the British found the trial unendurable.

He did prolong it for some time, and then, manoeuvring with his cavalry to turn Gough's right, compelled him to change position from west to north. Any change was a relief to the troops, and the appointed movements were executed with perfect steadiness and order. But the Sikh guns continued to play on Gough's infantry with terrible effect, and at length the gallant old man, conspicuous in the white coat which he always wore in action, galloped out alone with a single *aide-de-camp* to draw the fire upon himself. Meanwhile the Sikh cavalry bore down upon Gough's left, which was in echelon of squares upon the plain, approached to within one hundred and fifty yards, and halted. Gough ordered Whites brigade to charge; and the Third Light Dragoons, weak though they were in numbers and with horses that can hardly have been able to gallop, crashed into the stationary mass and forced it back.

Then, before anyone could realise what was going forward, the British cavalry re-formed column; and presently, together with the whole of the artillery, began to file away towards Ferozepore. The mad staff-officer, who had retreat to Ferozepore upon the brain, had been at work once more, and on this occasion to some effect. At about the same time, curiously enough, Tej Sing began to draw off his troops. He had learned something of the late action, and judged that if the British could capture such a position after such carnage, any attack upon them while defending that position must be hopeless. And thus after strange vicissitudes, at about four o'clock in the afternoon of the 22nd of December, the battle of Ferozeshah came finally to its end.

Gough's casualties in the two days amounted to twenty-four hundred and fifteen, of which nearly seven hundred were killed and seventeen hundred and twenty were wounded. Of the total number, twelve hundred and seven of the fallen were Europeans, including one hundred and fifteen officers, although the native cavalry regiments exceeded the British by six to one, and the native battalions present numbered fourteen against six British. Among the fallen officers were Wallace, Somerset—Hardinge's military secretary—and Broadfoot; while Brigadier-general Taylor and two more members of Hardinge's staff were wounded. Hardinge wrote a week after the action:

> Our native cavalry did not behave well. The Third Dragoons on every occasion behaved admirably, going through everything. . . . The British infantry, as usual, carried the day. I can't say I admire *sepoy* fighting.

On this testimony we can let rest the question who bore the brunt of Ferozeshah. The heroes of the action were beyond doubt the Third Light Dragoons. It is rare for cavalry to charge entrenched artillery; and only troopers of rare devotion and discipline would have faced such a trial. The Third had lost nearly one hundred men and over one hundred and twenty horses on the 18th of December; they lost one hundred and fifty-two more men and sixty more horses on the 21st; yet the remnant without hesitation charged and defeated superior numbers of Sikh cavalry on the 22nd. Few regiments of horse in the world can show a finer record of hardihood and endurance.

Of the infantry, the heaviest loss fell on the Ninth, who counted two hundred and eighty casualties; the Sixty-Second counting two hundred and sixty; the Hundred and Second two hundred and four; the Twenty-Ninth one hundred and eighty-four; the Thirty-First one hundred and forty-two; the Fiftieth one hundred and twenty-four; and the Eightieth eighty-one. This signified that in two actions, separated by only three days, the Ninth had suffered over three hundred and thirty casualties in action and the Thirty-First close upon three hundred. The native regiments which suffered most severely at Ferozeshah, as at Mudki, were the Second and Sixteenth Grenadiers.

The action has for many reasons been a subject of controversy, the chief point of debate being whether Hardinge were right or wrong in forbidding the attack until Littler had joined Gough, and whether Gough would have done better if he had been left to follow his own designs. Upon this it can only be said that, if a general's plans be overruled, and overruled moreover on the very point of execution, by superior authority, he cannot be held responsible for the consequences. Whether, as an abstract question of military expediency, Hardinge were right in forbidding the attack until the junction with Littler had been effected, men will probably debate until the end of time. Thereby he certainly caused much delay and sacrificed valuable hours of daylight; though, apart from Hardinge's intervention, much time seems to have been occupied to no great purpose before the attack was delivered. But it is not fair to blame a general for any miscarriage, if he have not a free hand to fight an action as he thinks best.

As to Gough's tactical handling of his troops, it is exceedingly hard to judge. His great initial difficulty was that his artillery was so inferior in numbers and weight of metal to that of the Sikhs that it was practically of value only, so to speak, as musketry of greater calibre and longer range. To all intent he was like a man who has to meet an enemy armed with an old-fashioned rifle, having himself only a fowling-piece. At a distance of five and twenty yards the one weapon is as deadly as the other; but the problem is how to close to within five and twenty yards without serious damage. The British round-shot did little or no mischief to the Sikh guns or their carriages, and the grape-shot was effective only so long as the fire could be maintained to drive the Sikh artillerymen from their guns. This was a very serious disadvantage; and Gough was really forced to throw all the brunt of the work upon the infantry.

Whether the infantry was manipulated in the best fashion, is another matter. Hardinge, (Rait, ii.), wrote that Gough disliked framing proper orders and looking to their execution; and this criticism seems to be confirmed by Harry Smith, who speaks of the army as "one unwieldy battalion under one commanding officer, who had not been granted the power of ubiquity." It should seem that Gough, having laid his plans for an assault upon the eastern face of the Sikh position—say two miles of entrenchment—did not modify them for the attack upon half that length of front; and hence the men crowded in upon the centre, putting the guns out of action and throwing each other into confusion. It is to be noticed, too, that when the British did break into the southern front, they were able to assail the batteries on the western and eastern fronts in flank, which shows that those batteries had not been moved. Wisdom after the event would therefore seem to suggest that, if Gough had made a demonstration with cavalry and horse-artillery upon one of the longer fronts, formed his infantry in greater depth and thrown them in successive waves upon the southern front, he would have accomplished his task with greater ease and much slighter loss. But it is very easy to fight a battle from an armchair; and Gough, after all, did but imitate the time-honoured methods of Monson and Wellesley. In any case he won a decided victory.

CHAPTER 4

Harry Smith Detached to Meet the Menace

On the 23rd of December, 1845, Hardinge rode into Ferozepore, where he met the cavalry and artillery marching out of the town, and had a stormy interview with the unfortunate staff-officer—still quite demented—who had ordered them away from Ferozeshah. The Sikhs, under Tej Sing, had recrossed the Sutlej by the ford of Sobraon; but Gough was powerless to follow them until his reinforcements should have arrived from Meerut, and his siege-train and stores of ammunition from Delhi. He therefore halted until the 24th, when he made a short march forward to Sultan-Khanwala, and on the 25th advanced to Arufka, about nine miles further to north and east, throwing out one division to Mallanwala, some six miles to the east and due south of Sobraon.

On the 6th of January the reinforcements began to come in, including the Ninth and Sixteenth Lancers, two regiments of native cavalry, two batteries of artillery, a company of sappers, the Tenth Foot and three native battalions. Therewith on the 12th Gough shifted his ground to eastward, so as the better to command the passages of the Sutlej, posting Harry Smith's division and Cureton's cavalry brigade on the right at Makhu, the main body in the centre over against the Sikh position of Sobraon, and the left at Attari, preserving communication with Ferozepore.

Meanwhile, the Sikhs, observing that Gough had been brought for the present to a standstill, detached some eight thousand men with seventy guns under Ranjur Singh, which marched up the north bank of the Sutlej to Phillaur, about six miles north of Ludhiana, established a bridge under cover of an old fortress there, and crossed the river

73

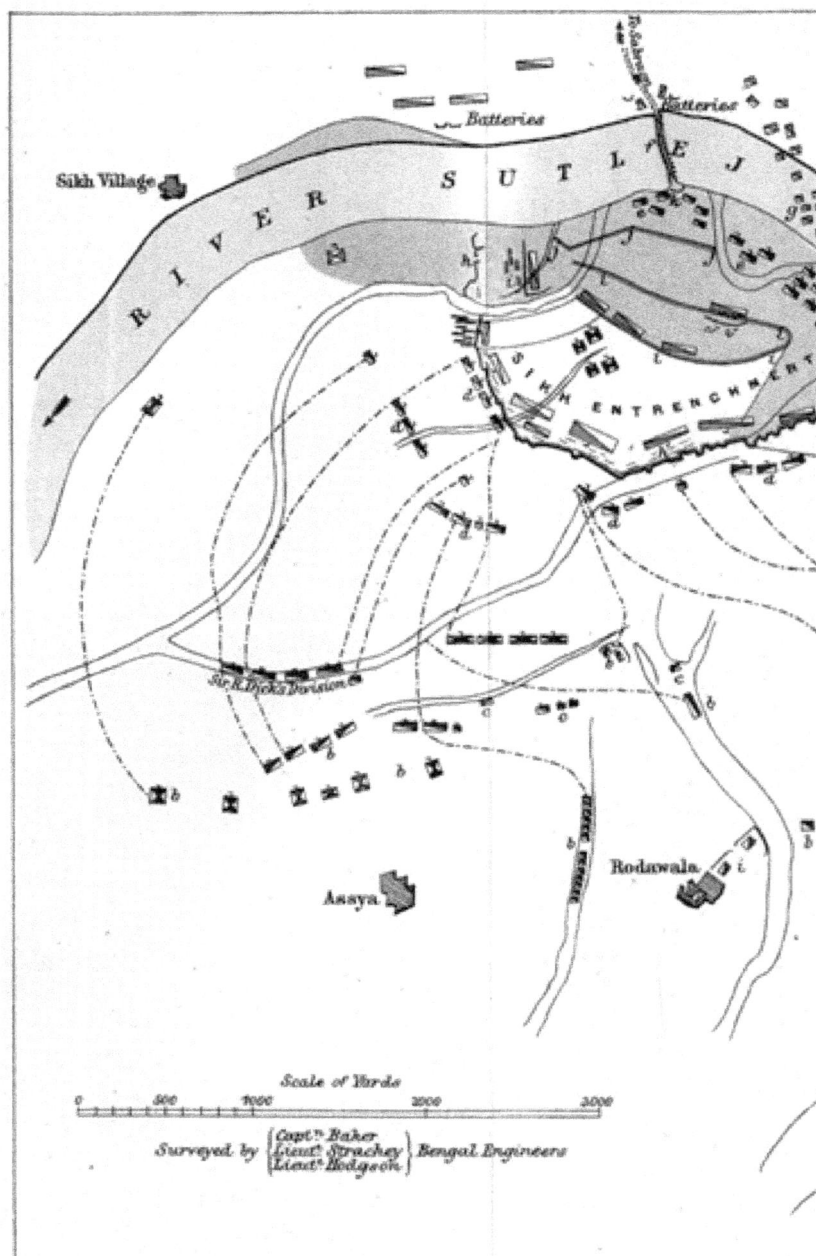

Sikh Village

Batteries

Batteries

R I V E R   S U T L E J

SIKH ENTRENCHMENT

Sir R. Dick's Division

Assya.

Rodawala.

Scale of Yards

0   500   1000   2000   3000

Surveyed by { Capt. Baker
Lieut. Strachey } Bengal Engineers
Lieut. Hodgson

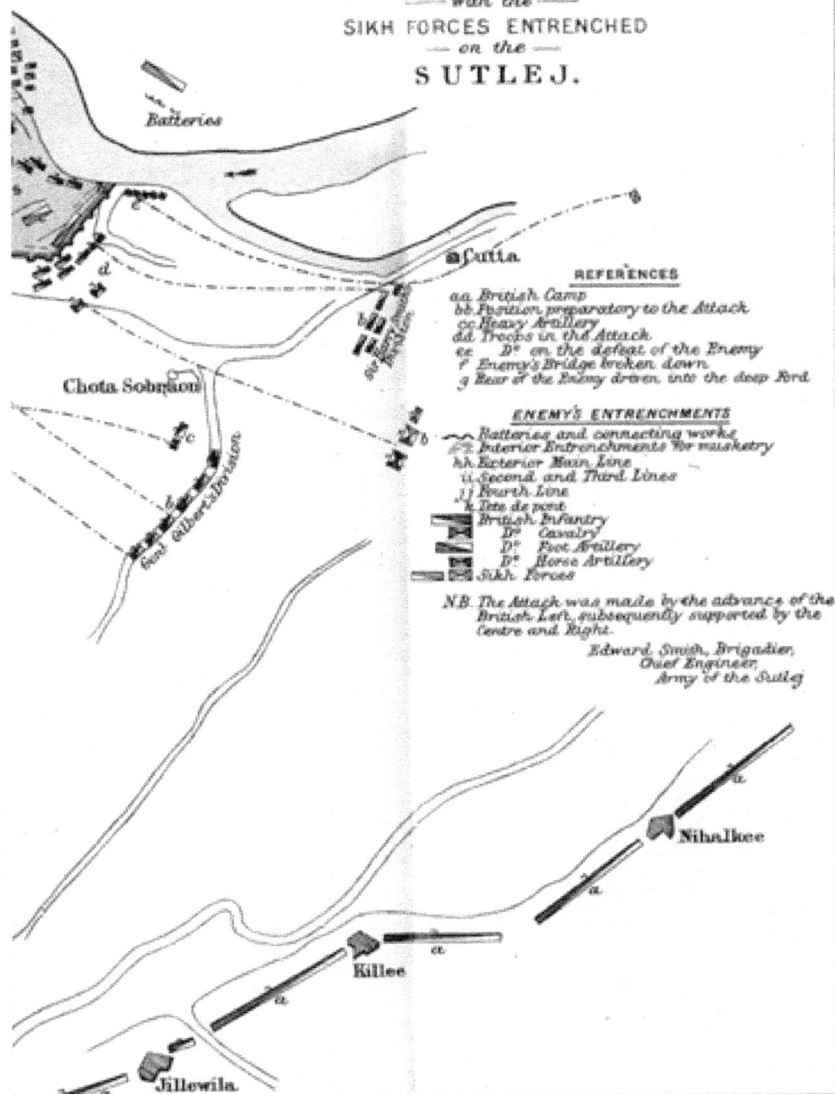

PLAN OF THE
BATTLE OF SOBRAON

FOUGHT ON THE 10TH FEBY 1846 BY THE BRITISH ARMY
under the personal command of

GENL SIR HUGH GOUGH, BART G.C.B.
—— with the ——

SIKH FORCES ENTRENCHED
— on the —
SUTLEJ.

Batteries

Cutta

REFERENCES

aa. British Camp
bb Position preparatory to the Attack
cc Heavy Artillery
dd Troops in the Attack
ee   Do on the defeat of the Enemy
f Enemy's Bridge broken down
g Rear of the Enemy driven into the deep Ford

ENEMY'S ENTRENCHMENTS

Batteries and connecting works
Interior Entrenchments for musketry
hh Exterior Main Line
ii Second and Third Lines
jj Fourth Line
k Tete de pont
British Infantry
   Do   Cavalry
   Do   Foot Artillery
   Do   Horse Artillery
Sikh Forces

N.B. The Attack was made by the advance of the
British Left, subsequently supported by the
Centre and Right.

Edward Smith, Brigadier,
Chief Engineer,
Army of the Sutlej

Chota Sobraon

Genl Gilbert's Division

Nihalkee

Killee

Jillewila

to threaten Gough's communications. They also threw garrisons into two small forts, Dharmkot and Fatehgarh, the one about twenty-five miles and the other about twelve miles to east of Gough's position and on the road between it and Ludhiana; and under cover of these they began to draw supplies from the left bank of the river, and to carry them over to the right bank. On the 16th, therefore, Gough ordered Harry Smith to take a brigade of infantry, a battery and two regiments of native horse to clear the enemy out of these strongholds; and Harry Smith, marching two hours before daylight of the 17th, found Fatehgarh abandoned. Pushing on at once to Dharmkot he reached it with his cavalry by 2 p.m., and after firing a few cannon-shot, received its surrender.

Halting for a day after this long march, he received a further message from Gough that on the 19th he would be reinforced by additional cavalry and artillery, which would augment his force to the total strength of three regiments of horse, including the Sixteenth Lancers, and eighteen guns, besides his original brigade of infantry. With these he was ordered to move on Jagraon, some eighteen miles to south-east of Dharmkot, thence open communication with Bassian, ten miles to south, upon which place the battering train and an immense convoy were marching to join Gough; and above all he was to open communication with Ludhiana itself, twenty-six miles to the north-east, for Ranjur Singh was within seven miles of it though still on the north bank of the Sutlej. At Bassian he would find the Fifty-Third Foot; at Ludhiana there was a garrison of one regiment of native cavalry, one battalion of native infantry, two Gurkha battalions and four guns, under Colonel Godby. All of these Smith was empowered to take under his command.

Smith accordingly, on the 19th, marched for Jagraon where he arrived on the 20th and picked up the Fifty-Third, which he had ordered to meet him there. The intelligence received at this place indicated that Ranjur's force was still between Phillaur and Ludhiana, some thirty miles away, but that the enemy had occupied two forts, Baddowal, about eighteen miles to the north-east, and a little to south of the main road to Ludhiana, and Gangrana, about ten miles due south of Baddowal, and had cavalry at both places. Unwilling to give these parties the chance of annoying him on both flanks, Smith decided to move on Ludhiana by the road north , of Baddowal, and sent repeated instructions to Godby to meet him with every man that he could spare at Suneth, about midway between Baddowal and Ludhiana. Leaving all wheeled transport and heavy baggage at Jagraon under the guard of two companies of native infantry, Smith resumed his march by moonlight at half-past twelve on the morning of the 21st, and by sunrise was within two miles of Baddowal.

Here a message reached him from Godby that Ranjur had marched from the vicinity of Ludhiana to Baddowal with his whole force; and the villagers gave intelligence that his strength had been considerably increased. Smith had therefore to decide whether he would break through the Sikhs, who would certainly have prepared a position to stop him, or turn that position by a flank march and so make his way to Ludhiana. He had with him the Sixteenth Lancers, one regiment of regular and one of irregular horse, the Thirty-First, which had lost over three hundred officers and men at Mudki and Ferozeshah, the Fifty-Third, a young battalion, the Twenty-Fourth and Forty-Seventh Native Infantry, both very weak and further diminished by the two companies left at Jagraon, and eighteen guns, two-thirds of them light pieces of horse-artillery.

Ranjur was reported to have at least ten thousand men and forty guns, and he could rest one flank of his line on the fortress of Baddowal. Smith could hardly hope to force his passage through the enemy without very heavy casualties; and, if he failed, not only was he lost but Godby at Ludhiana was lost also. Rightly judging that the relief of Godby was a matter of vital importance to himself, to Gough, and indeed to British rule in India, he decided to strike south and so, moving round Baddowal at about two miles distance, to make his way thus to Ludhiana.

Changing the order of his march, so that a single word of command would wheel his force into line to the left in battle-array, he led his troops on through the deep sand; and the Sikhs speedily set themselves in motion parallel to him. Travelling on roads while Smith's men were toiling through the sand, their column soon outstripped Smith's, and presently they opened a heavy fire of cannon upon Smith's infantry. A few shot fell among the transport, throwing the drivers into panic; and the Sikhs, taking advantage of the confusion, attacked the baggage-train and succeeded in carrying off a great part of it, including the sick and wounded.

At one moment Ranjur pressed more closely, but was checked by the fire of Smith's guns, which were massed in rear; and then with great skill he drew out a line of seven battalions, with cannon in the intervals, across the rear of Smith's column, as if to attack in earnest.

Smith willingly took up the challenge, and would have assailed this line had not his infantry been utterly exhausted. The cavalry and guns were therefore formed to screen the infantry, which gradually drew off in echelon of battalions until it had passed the village, Cureton manoeuvring his three regiments of horse with admirable skill to cover the movement.

The enemy dared not leave the village to encounter Smith in the open, and the column pursued its way unmolested to Ludhiana, the cavalry not coming in till 4 p.m., after sixteen hours under arms. The day had been intensely hot, and the fatigue of the infantry was such that many men were brought in on the horses of the troopers, or dragged into camp clinging to their stirrup-leathers. Some four hundred were missing, including those who had fallen in action, and though some two hundred straggled in during the next day or two, there was no doubt that the sick and prisoners would most of them be murdered. Altogether the men were disheartened and dispirited by the result of the day's work. (See Reynard's *History of the Sixteenth Lancers*).

Meanwhile not a sign had been found of Godby. He had been very urgent in his cries for relief, but had not held his troops ready for action; and on receiving Smith's instructions, he seems to have been slow and supine, for he did not move off until the firing began, and then, not knowing of Smith's change of route, took the wrong direction, ultimately returning to Ludhiana without firing a shot. However, after all Smith had effected his junction with him, and moreover, now lay across Ranjur's direct line of communication with Phillaur, compelling him to rely on a ford further down the Sutlej. Smith gave his men a day's rest, making every preparation to attack Ranjur at Baddowal; but Ranjur with sound judgement evacuated the place and marched northward towards the river, to meet reinforcements which were on their way to him.

Smith, therefore, on the 23rd marched back to Baddowal and occupying it, halted there for some days; for Gough had ordered Wheeler's brigade, two regiments of native cavalry and four guns, to reinforce him from his own camp, besides the Shekawati brigade from Bassian, and had further directed Taylor's brigade to advance to Dharmkot and remain there in reserve. This last Smith ordered to return, feeling himself strong enough without them, for Godby had marched in on the 24th, leaving Ludhiana under a guard of invalids, and Wheeler on the 26th. Smith had now some twelve thousand men, (see list following),

Battle of Sobraon

with thirty-two guns under his command, and, after giving Wheelers troops a day's rest, was ready to take the offensive.

★★★★★★

Cavalry: Brigadier-General Cureton.

> Macdowell's Brigade: 16th Lancers, 3rd Bengal L.C., 4th Irregular Cav.
>
> Stedman's Brigade: Gov.-gen.'s Bodyguard, 1st and 5th Bengal L.C., Shekawati Cav.

Horse Artillery: (Major Laurenson) 3 batteries.

Infantry:

> 1st Brigade: H.M. 31st Foot; 24th and 47th Bengal N.I.
>
> 2nd „ Wheeler—H.M. 50th Foot; 48th Bengal N.I., Sirmur Battn. of Gurkhas.
>
> 3rd „ Wilson—H.M. 53rd Foot; 30th Bengal N.I.
>
> 4th „ Godby—36th Bengal N.I., Nasiri Battn. of Gurkhas.

2 Field batteries, 2 eight-inch howitzers.

★★★★★★

His information was that Ranjur, after picking up a reinforcement of four thousand men—good soldiers trained by General Avitabile—would at dawn of the 29th move either on Jagraon, on Baddowal or on Ludhiana. Marching therefore at dawn of the 29th Smith struck north-westward, his cavalry in advance in contiguous columns of squadrons of regiments, with two batteries of horse-artillery in the intervals between brigades. In rear of the horse marched the infantry in contiguous columns of brigades at intervals of deploying distance, the open spaces being filled by artillery. A regiment of native cavalry was sent out wide to the eastward to watch for any hostile movement towards Baddowal or Ludhiana; but a spy, coming in two or three hours after the start, reported the Sikh Army to be advancing on Jagraon.

A march of eight or ten miles brought the force to the village of Porrain, at the top of a sandy ridge, and Smith, ascending to the roof of a house, caught sight of his enemy. At the foot of the ridge on which he stood was a level plain some two miles long and one mile wide; beyond it on a gentle rise were two villages, Aliwal, which was fortified, opposite his right, and Bhundri, masked only by a thin grove of trees on his left; and between the two ran a curved line of entrenchments. The Sikhs were in motion, apparently heading for Jagraon, but at the sight of Smith's array they halted and occupied both villages and the entrenchment. Deploying his cavalry into line Smith continued his advance, and presently found himself clear of the sand and upon firm, grassy land.

Therewith he ordered his two cavalry brigades to wheel off right and left so as to clear his front, and then deployed his infantry. Two brigades, Wheeler's on the right, Wilson's on the left, were in front line; echeloned in rear of them were Godby's brigade on the right and the Shekawati brigade on the left; and echeloned again well in rear of these were the two brigades of cavalry, Cureton's on the right and Macdowell's on the left. In this order Smith advanced as if on parade. Observing presently that his array was outflanked by the Sikh left, he wheeled his lines into column, took ground to his right, once again wheeled the columns into line and continued the forward movement. The sun shone brightly; there was no dust; every manoeuvre was perfectly executed; and the twelve thousand men acted as one. Rarely has there been a more stately prelude to a general action.

The British were apparently from six to seven hundred yards from the enemy when the Sikh guns opened fire from the whole length of their entrenchments. The shot at first fell short, but soon reached the British ranks as they marched forward; and Smith, now for the first time able to see something of what was before him, halted, in order to reconnoitre the enemy's position. The Sikhs had made the grave mistake of accepting battle with a river in their rear; and it was for Smith to take advantage of it. He decided first to bring up his right and carry the village of Aliwal, and, this done, to make a general attack on the Sikh centre and left.

Summoning Godby's brigade, therefore, from the right rear, he launched it, together with Hicks's brigade, against Aliwal and mastered it with little difficulty or loss, capturing two heavy guns. Therewith Smith ordered a general attack upon the Sikh centre and left, and Wheeler was soon hotly engaged. Ranjur, realising that his left was in extreme danger, if not actually turned, brought forward a large body of cavalry to cover the re-establishment of his position in that quarter; but these were instantly charged by Cureton and driven back in disorder upon their infantry.

Determined to press his advantage to the utmost, Smith called the Shekawati brigade to the support of Cureton, and, being now on the summit of the high ground, he perceived the enemy's camp alongside the river to be full of infantry, and turned Godby's brigade against their left flank and rear Godby carried everything before him; and

16th Lancers at Aliwal

Ranjur now realised that his retreat by the fords of the river was seriously menaced.

He therefore endeavoured to save himself by throwing back his left, and re-forming his line at right angles to the river, using the village of Bhundri, which was strongly fortified, as a pivot. To cover this manoeuvre he again brought forward a body of horse, to counter which Macdowell sent against them a squadron of the Third Light Cavalry with another of the Sixteenth Lancers in support. The native regiment hesitated, whereupon the squadron of the Sixteenth, under Captain Bere, charged without them, crashed into the Sikhs and rode through and through them, hunting the fugitives towards the river. Rallying his men Bere returned to find his way blocked by Sikh infantry, who threw themselves into squares, or rather equilateral triangles, and received him with a volley at short range.

In another minute the lancers had broken into them, and, though the Sikhs threw away their muskets and fought fiercely with sword and shield, they were utterly broken. Simultaneously another squadron of the Sixteenth, under Captain Fyler, rode down another block of Sikh infantry, and the two squadrons re-formed and rallied together.

Meanwhile Smith had thrown the two remaining squadrons of the Sixteenth, under Major Smyth, against an entrenched Sikh battery; and Smyth, galloping on under a terrific cannonade, captured every gun. The Sikh infantry in rear of the battery, after firing to the last, did not await the attack of the lancers, but boldly advanced to meet them with the sword, and closed with them in a bloody and determined struggle. These Sikh battalions, trained by Avitabile, fought, in fact, most gallantly; but the British infantry now came up to second the cavalry; and the village of Bhundri was cleared by the Fifty-Third. Then two batteries of horse-artillery came up to complete the discomfiture of the Sikh foot. A last gallant band, from eight hundred to a thousand strong, which had rallied under shelter of the bank of a ravine, was dislodged by a flanking charge of the Thirtieth Native Infantry and blasted out of existence by the fire of twelve guns at close range.

The entire Sikh force was in flight towards the ford by their camp, and in their rear and on both their flanks the British hemmed them in closer and closer, tearing them to pieces with their guns as they streamed away to the river. Ranjur had nine pieces unlimbered to cover the ford, but they were only fired once before the pursuers were upon them. Then the fugitives plunged into the river and into such boats as they had, in utter disorder under a tempest of shot and shell from the

Z

Y Z

From
Sultan Khanwallah

F D

D

F

E

X

E

F S

From Ferozpoor

A Maj. Gen. Littler Brig. Wallac

Brig. Harriot

Brig. Gough The Gov Ge

M

BRITISH.

AA British Army formed for Attack, Dec. 21st.

BB Bivouac of 2nd Division with Details on morning of 22nd.

C Sir H. Smith with 1st Brigade of Reserve, up to 3 a.m. on morning of 22nd.

DD British position after capture of enemy's camp on 22nd.

EE Final Position of British troops on 22nd.

FF Cavalry movement against enemy's final movement.

From Ferozpoor

Line of Advance of Sir

SIKHS.

XX Enemy's position on Dec. 21st.
YY First attack of enemy, Mid-day 22nd.
ZZ Final movement of enemy on 22nd.

1000 5

BATTLE OF FEROZESHAH,
DEC. 21 & 22, 1845

British cannon. Ranjur tried to bring away some of his guns, but two only reached the opposite bank, two more being left in mid-stream, and yet other two swallowed up by quicksands. He tried also to form some kind of line on the opposite bank, but this was speedily dissolved by a salvo from every piece of Smith's artillery. The Sikh host was driven headlong across the river in abject flight, with the loss of camp, baggage supplies, stores, and every one of their sixty-seven cannon.

Thus brilliantly did Harry Smith end his little campaign, having accomplished as awkward a task as is often set to a general. For he was sent out with a small force to secure communication in one direction with Bassian, the route by which Gough's siege-train must arrive from Delhi and Ferozepore, and in another direction with Ludhiana, and in each place to collect a handful of troops which might help him to engage a greatly superior enemy. Ranjur Singh showed good judgement when he posted himself at Baddowal, threatening both Smith and Godby like a king between two pieces on a draught-board; and it speaks ill for the Sikh cavalry that they did not give Smith a great deal more trouble on the 21st.

Then hardly had Smith arrived at Ludhiana than he had to rush back to Jagraon to pick up Wheeler's detachment, which by itself stood in danger of being overwhelmed. In fact he had to career about the triangle contained by Dharmkot, Ludhiana and Bassian, each side of it, roughly speaking, twenty-five miles long, gathering together detachments in the presence of a concentrated enemy. When at last he had all his men under his hand, he lost no time in marching to the attack.

With what numbers Ranjur Singh met him at Aliwal it is impossible to say. Smith speaks of thirty thousand men, others of forty thousand, but probably it is safest to take the lower figure and divide it by two. He had the good fortune not to find his enemy in so carefully prepared a position as Mudki and Ferozeshah, and he hit the weak point at once. Having struck it, he concentrated eight of his eleven battalions and three of his six regiments of horse upon the enemy's left, leaving Wheeler's three battalions and Macdowell's three cavalry regiments to deal with his centre and right.

The result was that the losses of Wheeler and Macdowell alone made up more than three-fifths of the casualty list, and the Sixteenth Lancers alone made up more than one-fourth of it. Their charges of two isolated squadrons first, then of the two remaining squadrons acting together, and finally of the whole regiment, were the most brilliant feature of the action; and Harry Smith seems to have timed them

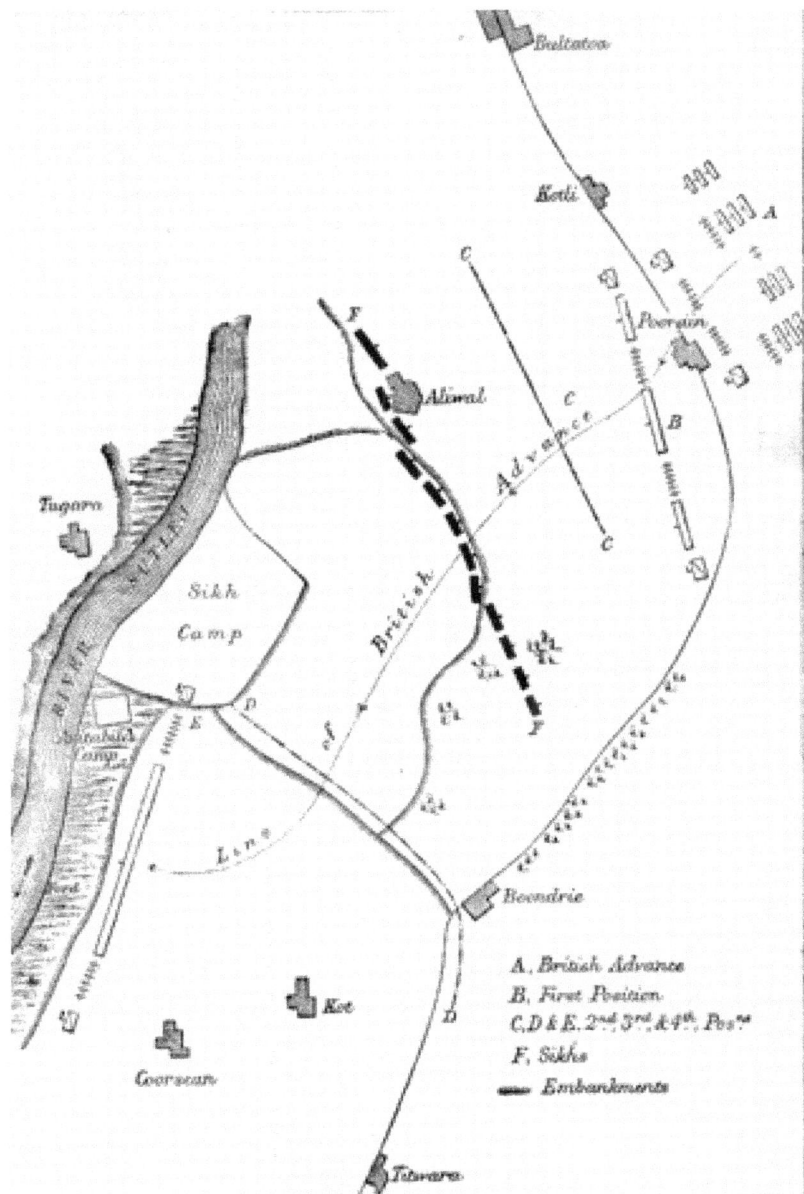

Bultutee

Kotli

A

Poorain

C

C

Advance

C

Aliwal

B

C

Tugara

Sikh

Camp

British

D

Constable
Camp

E

Ford

Lane

Boondrie

Kot

D

Goorsean

A, British Advance
B, First Position
C, D & E. 2nd, 3rd, & 4th, Pos.^{na}
F, Sikhs
Embankments

Tutwara

BATTLE OF ALIWAL

perfectly, so as to shatter Ranjur Singles last hopes of maintaining the fight.

In fact it was a masterly stroke, but it cost the regiment the price of one hundred and forty-four officers and men, fifty-eight of whom were killed outright. Of the other troops engaged the Fiftieth suffered the most heavily, but their casualties did not exceed seventy-three; and indeed those of the whole force amounted only to five hundred and eighty-nine, one-third of them killed. The Sikhs admitted a loss of three thousand killed. Putting the Sixteenth Lancers aside, it is seldom that casualties are so evenly distributed among all units as those of Aliwal; and the point held up by the Duke of Wellington to especial admiration was Harry Smith's utilisation of all three arms to the greatest possible advantage of each. Altogether Aliwal was a well-managed little affair.

The moral effect of the victory was very great. Mudki and Ferozeshah had been costly successes, the latter not very far removed from failure, and the *sepoys* shrank more and more from meeting the Sikhs. Now, however, the dreaded enemy had been not only defeated but harried, hunted and humiliated. To Gough, who with good reason had been miserably anxious about Harry Smith's expedition, the news of Aliwal, first heralded by the sound of the guns, came as an untold relief. He was, we are told, "nearly frantic with joy," but instantly restrained himself, and fell humbly on his knees to give God the glory. His situation was now much easier. The Sikhs had at once evacuated all their posts south of the Sutlej except their fortified position at Sobraon; his communications were secure, and the safe arrival of his siege-train was assured. On the 3rd of February, Feb. Harry Smith, having with much trouble disposed of his captured guns, marched back to rejoin the army, and reaching it on the 8th was enthusiastically received by all ranks. On the 9th Gough summoned his subordinate commanders to explain to them his plan of attack.

The position of the Sikhs at Sobraon was formidable. It consisted of a strongly fortified enceinte, containing a kind of inner citadel, skilfully adjusted to a re-entrant bend of the river. The southern front was about a mile and three-quarters long, the eastern front about half-a-mile, and the western about a mile, both of the last abutting northward upon the Sutlej. A bridge of boats connected this work with the northern bank, which was higher than the southern, and on this northern bank works had been constructed to enfilade not only the northern egress from the bridge, but also the eastern and western

BATTLE OF FEROZESHAH

fronts. In rear of these upon commanding ground was arrayed the force not required to hold the entrenchments, with numerous artillery. To put matters briefly, the Sikhs were drawn up in rear of a very broad and impassable ditch, with a strongly fortified outwork on the other side of that ditch, which outwork, together with all the approaches to it, was commanded by the main position. The vice of such a disposition is obvious enough; but none the less the problem of a successful attack upon it was not easy of solution.

As there were plenty of boats at Ferozepore, Hardinge suggested that these should be used to carry the bulk of the infantry and fifty guns over the river, under cover of darkness, to Ganda Singhwala, on the opposite bank, and that this force, moving up the northern bank, should fall upon the flank of the main Sikh position by surprise, seize the commanding ground, and so render the outwork untenable. Gough objected to this plan on the ground that such a flanking movement would lay open his communications; and Hardinge did not press it. There was nothing for it, therefore, but a direct attack; and it was hoped that since the siege-train was on the spot and Gough had now fifteen thousand men, (see list following), under his hand, the task would not strain his resources to excess.

★★★★★★

Cavalry Division: Major-general Sir Joseph Thackwell.

    1st Brigade: (Scott) H.M. 3rd L.D.; 4th and 5th Bengal
                      L.C., 9th Irregular Cav.

    2nd   ,, (Campbell) H.M. 9th Lancers; 2nd Irregular Cav.

    3rd   ,, Gov.-gen.'s Bodyguard.

    4th   ,, (Cureton) H.M. 16th Lancers; 3rd Bengal L.C.,
                      4th Irregular Cav.

Artillery:

    9 Horse-artillery batteries.

    3 Field-artillery nine-pounder batteries.

    2 Field-artillery twelve-pounder batteries.

    6 eighteen-pounders.

    18 heavy howitzers and mortars.

Infantry:

    1st Division. Harry Smith.

        1st Brigade Hicks. H.M. 31st; 47th Bengal N.I.

        2nd   ,, Penny. H.M. 50th; 42nd Bengal N.I.,
                      Nasiri Battn.

2nd Division: Gilbert.

      3rd Brigade Taylor. H.M. 29th; 41st and
              68th Bengal N.I.

    4th   ,, Maclaren. 1st Bengal Europ. (102nd);
              16th N.I., Sirmur Battn.

3rd Division: Dick.

      5th Brigade Ashburnham. H.M. 9th; H.M. 62nd;
              26th N.I.

    6th   ,, Wilkinson. H.M. 80th; 33rd and 63rd N.I.

    7th   ,, Stacey. H.M. 10th; H.M. 53rd; 43rd
              and 59th N.I.

Detached Brigade. 4th, 5th and 73rd N.I.

★★★★★★

The artillery officers declared at first that eighteen heavy howitzers and five eighteen-pounders would in an hour or two render the outwork untenable, and clear the way for a successful assault by infantry; but after closer examination of the fortifications they changed their opinion and pronounced such an attack to be impracticable. Dissatisfied with this report Hardinge consulted Major Henry Lawrence, the political agent, who had been originally in the artillery, and Major Abbott of the Engineers, who—such is human nature—disagreed with their colleagues and advocated the attack. Gough was, therefore, free to fight, as he wished, a general action.

He decided that the western front offered the most favourable point for attack, and he accordingly massed nineteen out of his twenty-four heavy pieces, including the whole of his eighteen-pounders, over against the south-western angle, assigning to Dick's division the duty of the assault. The centre, or southern front, was assigned to Gilbert's division, and the right, or eastern front, to Harry Smith's, the remainder of the heavy guns being posted between these two divisions opposite the south-eastern angle.

Of the cavalry, Scott's brigade was drawn up in rear of Dick, who was further supported by three battalions of native infantry; and Campbell's brigade was posted in rear of Harry Smith's division. Cureton's brigade was detached to make a diversion by simulating an attempt to cross the Sutlej at Harike, about three miles up the river from Sobraon. The batteries of field- and horse-artillery extended the heavy batteries into a semicircle embracing the greater part of the perimeter of the enemy's works, the light howitzers being massed off the south-eastern angle at the village of Chota Sobraon.

★★★★★★

It is impossible to say how many guns Gough had with him. There were too few gunners for the heavy ordnance, so those of three, if not four, horse-batteries were borrowed, and these batteries were left in camp. When the ammunition for the heavy pieces failed, Hardinge sent for these horse-batteries which were brought up by their drivers only, picked up their gunners and came into action late. See *Buckle*.

★★★★★★

At three o'clock on the morning of the 10th the troops got under arms in silence and moved off to their appointed positions. A dense mist forbade all operations for some hours, but by 6.30 a.m. it had cleared, and therewith the whole of the British artillery opened fire. The cannonade was not as effective as it should have been. The shells thrown by the mortars burst in the air, their fuses being too short; the eighteen-pounders were emplaced at too long range to do much damage; and, as a climax, after two hours' firing the ammunition of the heavy pieces failed. Gough complained that his orders as to the supply had not been obeyed; the gunners retorted that insufficient time had been allowed them for preparation; and, since the siege-train only reached Gough's camp on the 8th, the plea may be justified. Whatever the cause, ammunition failed, and at about 8.30 Gough was informed that the heavy pieces must cease fire.

The gallant old man received the news in a fashion which effectively banished any discouragement in the army. "Thank God," he cried to the officer who brought the unwelcome message, "then I'll be at them with the bayonet," and he ordered Dick's division to attack at once. Then came a curious incident. An officer arrived with a message from Hardinge at Ferozepore to the effect that, if Gough did not feel confident of success without great loss, he had better withdraw the troops and work up to the enemy's entrenchments by regular approaches. It seems that this officer, though a brave and honourable man, was incapable of comprehending the true purport of any order, for he had made a similar mistake on the night of the first day of Ferozeshah.

Hardinge's actual message was that, if Sir Hugh doubted the issue, he might exercise his discretion, but that if he only apprehended severe loss, he might go on. Even this might well have been spared to a commander-in-chief who had already begun his action; but the false message was delivered in its, stead, and, moreover, was thrice repeated. Gough, losing patience at last, silenced the messenger with the words:

Tell Sir Robert Dick to move on, in the name of God!

Accordingly at 9 a.m., Dick opened his attack with Stacey's brigade in line, the Tenth being on the right, the Fifty-Third on the left, with the Forty-Third and Fifty-Ninth Native Infantry between them. On their flanks two field-batteries and one horse-battery galloped out to successive positions until they closed to within three hundred yards of the enemy's heavy guns. The fire of the Sikhs from cannon, wall-pieces and muskets was terrific, but Stacey's brigade, moving steadily forward, stormed the entrenchments and drove the Sikhs in confusion from their guns upon the inner entrenchments.

Then speedily the enemy recovered themselves and, being in great force, counter-attacked with the greatest determination. Gough ordered Wilkinson to the support of Stacey, and Ashburnham to the support of Wilkinson, and directed Gilbert and Smith to throw out their light troops and make demonstrations along the whole length of the Sikh entrenchments. The Sikhs took not the slightest notice of these feints, but turned all their efforts against Dick. Gradually the three brigades were forced back, disputing every inch of ground, but unable to maintain themselves, until the Sikhs finally drove them from their batteries and recaptured their guns. The assault of Dick's division had failed, and therewith Gough's original plan of action had been brought to naught.

He had no alternative but to convert the feints of Gilbert and Smith into real attacks; and the Sikhs, relieved from the pressure upon their right, flew to their centre and left to take up the challenge. "Good God, they'll be annihilated," exclaimed Gough, as he watched Gilbert's men preparing for the assault. His forebodings were justified. Taylor's and Maclaren's brigades, rushing forward to the ditch, found the rampart too high to be ascended without scaling ladders, and were driven back with heavy loss, Taylor and Maclaren being both of them killed. A second attempt equally failed; and on the extreme right Harry Smith had fared little better. In that quarter Hicks's brigade led the assault, and was thrice driven back with heavy loss, the Thirty-First, weak through its casualties in former actions, losing one hundred and fifty men.

Harry Smith was ready with Penny's brigade to restore the fight; and the steadiness of the Fiftieth, which formed fours, as if on parade, to allow the shattered fragments of Hicks's brigade to pass through them, and as calmly re-formed line, all under heavy fire, was enough to give any commander confidence. But it was all that Smith could do for half-an-hour to hold his own within the enemy's entrenchments, and for a full hour the issue of the fight was in the gravest doubt.

But the distraction of the Sikhs from their right to their centre and left had enabled Dick's men to rally and renew their attack with success; and Gilbert's brigades, making another assault, at last penetrated into the entrenchments, the men hoisting each other up to the embrasures in default of ladders. Finally, on the enemy's right the sappers cleared a way over ditches and parapets, and Thackwell, passing his cavalry in single file into the entrenchments, let loose the Third Light Dragoons, who once again galloped over batteries and field-works, cutting down all who dared to withstand them.

Then the Sikhs began to give way, slowly and stubbornly, yielding to steady pressure from three sides, which forced them back upon their bridge of boats. By a strange fatality the Sutlej had risen seven feet in the night, so that the fords were impassable, and the centre boat of the bridge—whether to check pursuit or to force the Sikhs to fight by denying them retreat— had been removed. Many grey-bearded old chiefs stood up to the last, waving their swords, and were killed; many of their men nobly emulated their example; but at last came the inevitable rush for the bridge. The Sikh cavalry had cut up the British wounded as they lay on the ground, and the victors were in no mood of mercy. The sides of the bridge gave way, and the fugitives were driven by thousands into the water, where the British guns played on them relentlessly with grape and shrapnel. Before noon the action was over. From eight to ten thousand Sikhs had perished; every gun of theirs had been captured; and the power of the arrogant Khalsa had been broken.

The casualties in Gough's force amounted to two thousand two hundred and eighty-three of all ranks, of whom three hundred and twenty were killed. Among these last were Sir Robert Dick, a veteran of the Peninsula, and the Brigadiers Taylor and Maclaren; among the wounded were Gilbert and Brigadier-General Penny. The losses were far more evenly distributed among the British and the Indian battalions than in any previous action of the war, for the *sepoys* had learned the lesson of Aliwal and fought well. It was in Harry Smith's division that the difference between the two was most strongly marked, for the Fiftieth counted two hundred and thirty-nine casualties, the Thirty-

First, who went into action only four hundred strong, one hundred and fifty-four, and the three native battalions put together, two hundred and twenty-three.

In Taylor's brigade of Gilbert's division, the Twenty-Ninth claimed one hundred and eighty-seven casualties out of four hundred and two, and in Maclaren's brigade the Hundred and Second one hundred and ninety-seven out of four hundred and ninety-five. The three brigades of Dick's division suffered most lightly of all, the Tenth counting one hundred and thirty-two killed and wounded, the Fifty-Third nearly as many, the Forty-Third Native Infantry just over one hundred, and the remainder all under, and most of them considerably under, one hundred. Nevertheless the *sepoys* did their duty, and the two battalions of Gurkhas greatly distinguished themselves. But for this fact Gough's assault at Sobraon would undoubtedly have failed.

It is difficult to know what judgement to pass upon the action. There was certainly mismanagement of the heavy artillery, particularly of the eighteen-pounders, which, if properly handled, should have levelled a great part of the enemy's entrenchments and dismounted at least some of their guns; but whether this were the fault of the chiefs of artillery or of Gough himself, it is impossible to say. Possibly the fact that Hardinge invoked junior officers of engineers and artillery to overrule the opinion of seniors did not make for hearty and united effort.

But Harry Smith declared further that Gough chose the wrong point of attack, and that, having chosen it, he massed insufficient troops before it to make the assault successful. There seems to be more point in the first part of this criticism than in the second, for Stacey's brigade appears to have gained its original footing in the Sikh entrenchments without any extraordinary effort, though the whole division failed to make that footing good. Harry Smith was undoubtedly the first to establish himself in the Sikh position; and to all intent his attack and that of Gilbert gave time to Dick's division to recover itself and make their second and successful attempt.

Not until both of these had carried the first line could either of Gilbert's brigades make the slightest impression; and this does not suggest a happy direction of the fight. But the storming of a fortified position defended by resolute troops and a powerful artillery must always be a hazardous business; and Gough was undoubtedly right in making a direct attack when his enemy was so incautious as to accept battle with an impassable river in his rear. Manoeuvring, such as that suggested by Hardinge, might have turned the Sikhs out of their position at Sobraon at less cost, if that operation be reckoned with alone; but the campaign would have been prolonged; and the sum total of casualties at its end might have exceeded those incurred by the single decisive action. Gough may have lost many men, possibly more than he ought, but he did end the war at a blow.

Directly that the battle was over Gough began to make his arrangements for crossing the Sutlej, and on the 12th and 13th the main body of the army passed the river, leaving three brigades of infantry and one of cavalry to escort the sick, the baggage and the sixty-seven guns captured from the Sikhs. On the night of the 12th Feb, the advanced guard occupied the fort of Kasur, some twelve miles northwest of Ferozepore; on the 13th the rest of the force moved up to them; and on the 14th Gholab Singh, a chief chosen because he had refused to join in hostilities against the British, arrived to negotiate for peace. Hardinge was ready enough to come to terms. The Sikh Army, though heavily punished, had not been annihilated, and they had safely brought away twenty-five guns which, during the action of Sobraon, had been in position on the north side of the river.

Complete conquest, to be followed by annexation, would have involved many sieges and a petty warfare which would have protracted operations into the hot season. Hardinge and Gough agreed that they could afford neither the men nor the money for such a campaign. Sir Charles Napier had collected twelve thousand men at Bahawalpur, and was thirsting for action. It was one of the great disappointments of his life that he had not been called to play his part in the war; but still Hardinge and Gough shrank from pressing their advantage. The truth seems to be that they did not feel too confident as to the result. The four actions of Mudki, Ferozeshah, Aliwal and Sobraon, alone had cost well over six thousand casualties, and of these over thirty-four hundred had fallen upon the Europeans.

Other petty affairs and sickness must have swelled that number to nearly four thousand; and the effective strength of the three British cavalry regiments and the eight British battalions with Gough can never have been above nine thousand. Practically, therefore, the European portion of the force had been reduced by nearly one-half, and the loss of officers had been specially severe. No doubt financial considerations also weighed heavily with Hardinge; but the military arguments in favour of peace were of themselves sufficiently cogent. It seems little of an exaggeration to say that Gough's soldiers had been fought to a standstill.

The terms laid down by Hardinge were the cession of the territory between the Beas and the Sutlej, known as the Jullundur Doab, and an indemnity of half-a-million sterling, or, as an equivalent, the districts of Kashmir and Hazara. Further, the Sikhs pledged themselves to yield up the twenty-five guns which they had succeeded in saving, and to restrict the numbers of their army to twenty-five battalions of infantry and twelve thousand cavalry. Within a few hours Gholab Singh accepted these conditions. On the 18th the army resumed its march on Lahore; on the 20th entered the Sikh capital; and on the 8th of March the treaty was signed. Hardinge received a viscounty and Gough a barony, each with a pension, for their services; and so ended, nominally, the First Sikh War.

CHAPTER 5

Siege of Multan

The treaty of Lahore had hardly been signed before difficulties began over its fulfilment. During the minority of the young *maharaja*, Dhulip Singh, the administration of the Punjab was necessarily entrusted to a Council of Regency, with Lal Singh at its head. It was represented that without the support of a British force this government would not last a week. Very reluctantly, and after repeated refusals, Hardinge consented to leave a wing of irregular cavalry, one horse-battery, two field-batteries, one European and eight native battalions at Lahore, under the command of Sir John Littler. This arrangement was supposed to last only till the end of 1846, but even so, Gough naturally condemned it as a dispersion of force. Military considerations, however, had to yield to political exigency; and, to make the best of a bad matter, Henry Lawrence was installed as resident, with his brother John in charge of the Jullundur Doab, and with his other brother George, Major Abbott, John Nicholson, Herbert Edwardes and Harry Lumsden, for colleagues or subordinates.

Then came difficulties over Kashmir. Hardinge had foreseen that the pecuniary indemnity would not be forthcoming; but, when Kashmir was surrendered in lieu of it, it was obvious that military occupation of a very difficult mountainous country three hundred miles from the Sutlej was out of the question. The Indian government could afford neither the men nor the money to hold Kashmir in force, and to lock up a brigade or any weak detachment in it would have been sheer madness. Hardinge, therefore, made over Kashmir to Gholab Singh for a payment of three-quarters of a million sterling. But the Sikh governor of the province refused to give it up until a mixed force of Sikhs and British under Henry Lawrence advanced against him, when he surrendered without firing a shot. It was then found that

Lal Singh and the *Rani* had abetted the recalcitrance of the Governor, and Lal Singh was, after due trial, deposed from his high office at the head of the Regency. Such incidents as these showed clearly that the withdrawal of the British garrison from Lahore would infallibly result in anarchy; and Hardinge offered the Sikh chiefs the alternative either of complete evacuation of Lahore by the Indian government, or of a British Protectorate during the remaining years of the *maharaja's* minority.

They declared unanimously for the Protectorate, and accordingly a new treaty was signed in December 1846. Thereby the *rani* was shorn of all power, in return for a pension; and a new Council of Regency was appointed to carry out the behests of the British resident. For twelve months the system worked well. Henry Lawrence was obliged to go home on sick leave at the end of 1847, when he was succeeded by Sir Frederick Currie. So successful had been Lawrence's administration that Hardinge confidently believed the problem of the Punjab to have been solved.

None the less he took military precautions, and for the greater safety of the north-west frontier he increased the total force at Meerut and to north-west of it to fifty thousand men with sixty guns. But, on the other hand, owing to financial pressure he, at the beginning of 1847, decided to reduce the native army by fifty thousand men, cutting down the establishment of battalions from one thousand to eight hundred, and of cavalry regiments from five hundred to four hundred and twenty. In the artillery he diminished the establishment of horses only, and he actually increased the amount of ammunition carried by each battery in its limbers and waggons.

He was careful, too, not to disband any existing regiments, actually adding eight new regiments of cavalry; but in the matter of reducing the strength of battalions he was, despite of Gough's protests, inexorable. Subsequent events were soon to prove that his policy was mistaken, but he was delivered from the burden of the consequences. In 1847 he resigned the position of Governor-General; and on the 12th of January 1848, there arrived as his successor at Calcutta a young man of thirty-five, James, Earl of Dalhousie.

Three months later came an unpleasant incident in the Punjab. In pursuance of the general work of improving the administration of the country two British officials, Mr. Vans Agnew of the Civil Service, and Lieutenant Anderson of the Bombay Army, were sent to Multan as resident magistrates. The Sikh governor, Mulraj, upon hearing of their

MULTAN FORTRESS

appointment, resigned his own; and they were accordingly accompanied by his chosen successor, Khan Singh. They arrived at Multan on the 18th of April and were most courteously received by Mulraj, but, when they took over the fort on the next day, they were both cut down by men of the garrison and severely, though not mortally, wounded. Vans Agnew contrived to send a report of this to Herbert Edwardes, at Dera Fateh Khan, some eighty miles to the north-west, on the same evening; but on the 20th the Sikh troops in the fort came out, murdered both officers, and exposed their mutilated bodies on the walls of Multan.

At the outset the incident seemed to be of no great importance. It was purely a political outrage, which might possibly have been provoked by tactless behaviour on the part of the officers; and accordingly the political agents rose like one man to call for an immediate advance of troops upon Multan. Herbert Edwardes, taking matters into his own hands, collected all the forces of the Sikh Regency that could be spared, appealed for help to the loyal chief of Bahawalpur, and actually moved upon the fortress. Before starting, he sent a message to Currie, the resident at Lahore, urging the peril which menaced Vans Agnew and Anderson; whereupon Currie ordered General Whish to march with such troops as could be spared from Lahore to Multan. He reported this proceeding to Gough, who approved his action; but Currie, presently learning that the officers had been killed, countermanded the movement of Whish and applied to Gough for instructions.

Meanwhile Edwardes, on the night of the 24th of April, crossed the Indus with a thousand Sikhs and six hundred Pathans, but, hearing in his turn that it was too late to save Vans Agnew and Anderson, as also that Mulraj intended to march against him, he returned to Dera Fateh Khan. His Sikhs were already mutinous, but he overawed them with his Pathans; and on the 4th of May he was joined by General van Cortlandt, with a battalion of Mohammedan infantry and a battery of horse-artillery, which he had summoned from Dera Ismail Khan. Thereupon Mulraj, who had followed Edwardes as far as Leiah, twenty miles from Dera Fateh Khan, retreated; and at this point Currie stepped in again.

Aware that few Sikh troops could be trusted to act against Mulraj, he decided to employ only those in which he thought he could confide. He arranged, therefore, that five columns should operate for the pacification of the Multan district, three of them composed of Sikh soldiers under Sikh commanders, of whom Shere Singh was the most

ASSAULT ON MULTAN

prominent, one of the troops collected by Edwardes, and the fifth of the levies of the Raja of Bahawalpur. Multan fortress itself he reserved to be dealt with by British troops. Needless to say, the Sikh troops did not appear; and Mulraj, leaving a small garrison in Multan, crossed the Chenab with six thousand men and thirteen guns. Edwardes, who was now again isolated from Van Cortlandt, marched in haste to join him, and, being reinforced from Bahawalpur, defeated Mulraj twice on the 18th of June and the 1st of July, and drove him under the walls of Multan. It was, however, ominous that of the three Sikh columns, which should have helped him, two had joined him with none but Mohammedan troops, the Sikhs having deserted, while Shere Singh waited within five miles of Multan, as if undecided which side to take.

Edwardes, young and flushed with success, meanwhile conceived the plan of besieging and taking Multan itself, and so putting an end to the rebellion. He only wanted a few heavy guns and mortars—so he airily declared—with Major Napier, the future Lord Napier of Magdala, as engineer to plan the operations. Strangely enough Napier pronounced himself in favour of this hare-brained scheme, naming a brigade of infantry with a few heavy guns, mortars and howitzers, as sufficient for the purpose. The political agents, including John and Henry Lawrence, all cried out that Multan was a place of no strength and could be easily mastered. But it lay with Gough to decide whether gunners should be allotted to Edwardes's siege-train; and Gough very firmly set his foot upon the whole design. Napier, on maturer consideration, revoked his previous opinion; and thus an enterprise which must have ended disastrously and brought about innumerable awkward complications, was happily arrested.

Since Edwardes's scheme of campaign had been quashed, Currie set on foot a new one of his own. On the 10th of July he ordered a British force, drawn from Lahore and Ferozepore, to move upon Multan with a siege-train duly equipped, under General Whish. He reported his proceedings to Gough, who pronounced the force too small, and increased it to two brigades of infantry, a native cavalry brigade, two troops of horse-artillery and a siege-train.

★★★★★★

Whish's Force:
  Cavalry Brigade: Lt.-Col. Salter—7th, 11th Irreg. Cav., 11th Light Cav.
  Artillery and Engineers: 2 troops horse-artillery, 4 cos. Foot-artillery, 3 cos. sappers, 2 cos. pioneers.

Infantry: 1st Brigade—Lt.-Col. Hervey—H.M. 10th Foot; 8th,
52nd Bengal N.I.

2nd Brigade—Lt.-Col. Markham—H.M. 32nd; 49th,
51st, 72nd Bengal N.I

★★★★★★

Accordingly the troops left Ferozepore and Lahore on the 24th of July; and the British regiments were sent down the Ravi and Sutlej by water while the native regiments marched along the banks, moving by night to avoid the heat. On the 18th and 19th of August the troops, (the 32nd did not come in until the 25th), encamped within three miles of Multan; on the 4th of September the siege-train arrived; and on the same day Whish summoned the fortress to surrender, and was answered by defiance.

Major Napier, the chief engineer, suggested two plans, the first to storm the town out of hand by a surprise attack from the south; and the second to move round to the citadel on the north and attack it by regular approaches. The first was prompted by the political desire for a speedy success, but was rejected as unduly costly and as indicating mistrust of success, for Edwardes had already thrown up batteries against the south front, where the enemy was entrenched outside the walls. Ground was broken on that side accordingly on the 6th; and by the 9th three batteries had been completed, one of two eight-inch howitzers, another of three eight-inch mortars, and a third of four eighteen-pounders.

On the 10th an attack was made on an outlying position by detachments of the Tenth Foot, and of the Forty-Ninth and Seventy-Second Native Infantry, which was repulsed with the loss of nearly one hundred men. Napier then threw up another battery of four five-and-a-half-inch mortars; and on the 12th of September Whish stormed the Sikh entrenchments, and drove the enemy back almost under the walls. Five hundred of the enemy were left dead on the ground; but Whish's casualties exceeded two hundred and fifty, seventy-four of them falling upon the Tenth and forty-nine upon the Thirty-Second, each of which regiments had furnished six companies for the assault. Half-a-mile of ground had been gained, but the actual leaguer of Multan had not even been begun; and even on the 9th Napier had expressed his opinion to Whish that his force was too weak to prosecute the siege.

Whish at first positively refused to listen to such gloomy counsel; but on the 14th he was staggered by the news that Shere Singh, who hitherto had seemed friendly and had been actively aiding Edwardes with his troops, had joined Mulraj in rebellion. This signified that the contest was not to be against a single recalcitrant chief, but with the whole strength of the Sikh nation. Apart from that, the actual composition of the garrison of Multan had altogether changed in a few weeks. Mulraj's irregular levies had been replaced by old Sikh soldiers, and it was reckoned that there were ten thousand of them in the city of Multan alone. In the circumstances it was hopeless to think of continuing the siege. Not only were the prospects of an assault hopeless, but the communications of the besieging force were gravely threatened. Napier reckoned that reinforcements of two more brigades would be needed to ensure success; and Whish, on the evening of the 15th, withdrew his troops to Sadusain, to secure his communications by ferry with Sind, Bombay and the country beyond the Indus on the one hand, and with Bahawalpur, Ferozepore and Lahore on the other.

So ended the campaign of the political agents, in waste of time, energy, money and lives, as is usual with the work of the amateur soldier. Let us now look to the views and actions of men who were genuinely of the military profession. When, upon certain intelligence that Vans Agnew and Anderson had been murdered, Currie sought instructions from Gough, the general decided without hesitation that an immediate advance of the army would be, from a military point of view, most unwise. No one knew what the outrage at Multan might portend. It might be a mere isolated, incident, in which case it could be dealt with at leisure by the Sikh government, for it was certain that nothing could bring the dead men to life again. But, on the other hand, it might be part of a preconcerted scheme of rebellion on the part of that same Sikh Government, or a symptom of its inability to hold its soldiers in check; and in that case the situation became in the highest degree serious.

An immediate advance might precipitate a second Sikh war; and this was an event upon which Gough reckoned as inevitable sooner or later, for he had never regarded the first war as decisive, and he had no trust in the good faith of the Sikh government. An advance, then, if made at all must be made in force; and Gough did not consider it safe to invade the Punjab with a smaller army than twenty-four thousand men with seventy-eight guns, added to a further reinforcement from Sind. Now the utmost strength that could be collected from the foremost stations, without reducing them to dangerous weakness, was ten thousand men and forty-eight guns; and these, owing to the system of granting furloughs to the native troops in the spring, could not be collected together before June. Even then there was another difficulty. There was no transport ready for these troops, the whole of their carriage having been, through motives of economy, discharged by the supreme government at Calcutta.

An immediate advance upon Multan, therefore, would mean the launching of an inadequate and imperfectly equipped force into active operations in the hottest season of the year in one of the hottest countries in the world. The district of Multan would be inundated by the melting of the Himalayan snows; proper investment of the city would be impossible; much time would be needed to bring up an adequate siege-train; and meanwhile the troops would die by hundreds of fever, sunstroke and heat-apoplexy.

So reasoned Gough with the wisdom born of sound thinking and long experience. It is true that he doubled the strength of the force required of him by Currie for General Whish; but, being unable to overrule the authority of the political agent, he could only do what he could to avert the worst consequences of Currie's folly. The Duke of Wellington at home confirmed Gough's judgement; and Dalhousie on the spot had the courage and good sense to support his policy against all the clamour of political ignorance and impatience. But Dalhousie was not so ready to second Gough's positive proposals for immediate preparation.

Foremost among the general's recommendations was one to restore the native regiments to the establishment which had ruled before Hardinge's ill-timed reductions, with the double object of gathering in twelve to fifteen thousand masterless old soldiers for the Company's army and of preventing them from taking service with the Sikhs. Dalhousie, while granting Gough full powers in minor matters, disapproved of his principal measures. He considered that twenty thousand men and a siege-train of the second class would be ample to meet all emergencies. He declined, on grounds of economy, to allow transport to be immediately collected, and above all he refused to sanction the re-enlistment of discharged *sepoys*, (Rait, *Life of Viscount Gough*, ii.).

Meanwhile signs had multiplied that a general rising of the Sikhs was imminent. Far to north Major George Lawrence, brother of Henry and John, was in charge of Peshawar, with Major James Abbott under him in control of the Hazara country to east of him. In July Abbott reported grave unrest among his Sikh garrisons, and his suspicions that Chattar Singh, father of Shere Singh, was the moving spirit in stirring it. In August Chattar Singh openly justified those suspicions by exciting a mutiny among the Sikh troops at Haripur, and sent emissaries to raise the Sikhs all over the country. In alarm for the safety of Attock, Abbott sent John Nicholson with a small force to hold that fort; and for some days he and Nicholson contrived by means of their native levies to cramp Chattar Singh's military activities, though they could not prevent him from sending appeals for aid to Shere Singh at Multan, to Dost Mohamed at Kabul, and to his brother, Sultan Mohamed at Kohat.

The situation was evidently critical; and both Lawrence and Nicholson, true to their character as political agents, but utterly forgetful of their training as soldiers, clamoured for a brigade to be sent up to Hazara. Gough flatly declined to fritter away his force by senseless and dangerous detachment of isolated brigades; Dalhousie supported him, and even Currie signified his agreement. As a matter of fact Gough had no troops to spare, for he had not yet, in the third week of August, received permission to collect a field-force upon the frontier.

At last, in the first days of September, Dalhousie recognised, as he put it, that financial must yield to military considerations; and he authorised Gough to collect a sufficient force both to support Whish's troops about Multan and to provide against any outbreak on the frontier. But he still declined to augment the establishment of the Bengal Army. Then came the news of the little check before Multan on the 9th of September, and Gough made arrangements for a force of cavalry to cross the Sutlej and for a brigade of infantry to proceed to Bahawalpur.

Shortly afterwards arrived the tidings of Shere Singh's defection, and then at last, on the 30th of September, Dalhousie ordered the augmentation of the regiments of the Native army to their old establishment, and sanctioned the summoning of troops, as Gough had proposed, from Sind and Bombay. Thus after more than four months of delay the general had his will; but meanwhile an appreciable detachment had been taken from his army and planted in the neighbourhood of Multan for no useful military purpose whatever.

The month of October saw difficulties multiplied. On the 9th Shere Singh quitted Multan with his own infantry and some of Mulraj's cavalry and marched up the Chenab to join the rebels of the north; neither Whish nor Edwardes moving a man to prevent him. On the 18th George Lawrence had a more or less successful skirmish with Chattar Singh in the Hazara country and forced him to retire towards Attock; but on the 23rd the Sikh troops at Peshawar broke into open mutiny, and Lawrence, with his brother officers, had to ride for their lives to Kohat. There Sultan Mohamed Khan, who had promised them protection, kept them for a time as his own prisoners, and later handed them over to the Sikhs at Peshawar. This gave Chattar Singh a reinforcement of six good regiments of infantry, a thousand cavalry and, to Gough's great indignation, thirty guns.

Lawrence, as he observed, must have known for months that this mutiny would certainly come, yet he made no attempt to render these guns unserviceable. Then the Sikh troops at Bannu mutinied, murdered their Mohammedan commander and an English officer, and on the 21st and 22nd marched to join Shere Singh, who had halted at Jhang. Shere Singh's next movement could not be divined, but there were fears, much derided by Gough, that he would march on Lahore. Meanwhile the irrepressible Currie had taken upon himself to send a brigade of infantry to the Jullundur Doab, where John Lawrence was hampered by some petty difficulties.

The mania among the political agents for ordering small detachments of troops here and there to serve their own immediate purposes presents a very curious pathological study. There were many good and able men among them who have left great reputations—the three Lawrences, Edwardes, Nicholson and others—and the great majority had begun life as soldiers. They knew, or should by this time have known, that there was a general rebellion of the Sikhs; but not one of them could look at any sphere of action except his own, nor conceive of military operations as a whole. Thus one and all seem to have held themselves entitled in any difficulty, whether or not of their own making, to the services of a brigade. Gough at length lost all patience, and on the 28th of October took the command of all troops absolutely into his own hands, even empowering his officers in advance to send back in irons to Lahore any political agent who tried to interfere with his arrangements, (Rait, ii.).

Shere Singh's menace to Lahore proved, as Gough had foreseen, to be a mere feint, his real movements pointing to Wazirabad, on the south side of the Chenab and one hundred and fifteen miles from Lahore. Gough looked upon this point as the key of the situation, and had wished to move an army thither in September, so as to overawe equally Kashmir, Peshawar and Multan; but he had not been allowed to collect an army, much less to occupy with it a strategical position.

SKETCH, AFTER TAKING THE CITY OF MOOLTAN, NEAR THE "CHUNDA CHOWK," OR GREAT BAZAAR.—JAN. 2, 1849

As things were, he could only send an advanced detachment of cavalry across the Sutlej to cover Lahore; and this force he strengthened and pushed across the Ravi, under command of General Cureton, on the 2nd of November. (H.M. 3rd Dragoons and 14th L.D., 8th Bengal N.C., 12th Irreg. Cav., 3 troops of horse-artillery; one light field-battery; Godby's Infantry Brigade—102nd Foot and 7th Bengal N.I.).

Cureton moved forward to Kela Dedar Singh, and there remained on the watch, being presently further reinforced by a second brigade of infantry, (Eckford's Brigade: 31st and 56th Bengal N.I.).

Troops were now moving rapidly from all quarters into Ferozepore, though the preparations of the Commissariat, owing to Dalhousie's delay in granting money, were very backward; and on the 6th of November Gough arrived there in person, intent upon a speedy advance. He was met by the tidings of the fall of Peshawar and the capture of Abbott's guns; but still more important news came in that Shere Singh, in his advance northward, had halted twenty-five miles short of Wazirabad at Ramnagar. This increased Gough's anxiety for an immediate forward movement, so as to make the Punjab the field of operations and engage Shere Singh there before he could join his father, Chattar Singh, in the far more difficult country about Peshawar.

Multan for the time Gough left out of account as a secondary matter. At present Shere Singh had only an advanced detachment at Ramnagar, communicating with his main force on the other bank of the Chenab by a ford. Gough hoped to entice the entire host across the river, beat them, and, through a rapid movement of his cavalry by way of Wazirabad, to cut them off from the revolted garrison of Bannu and the levies of Chattar Singh. In fact he entered upon his campaign with some hope of beating his enemy in detail, the great obstacle to his plans being that the Chenab lay between him and them. Cureton's detachment was thrown out as a bait to lure Shere Singh across the river; but, fearing to leave him too weak, Gough on the 8th ordered Colin Campbell to draw a strong brigade from Lahore, cross the Ravi, join Cureton and take the whole detachment under his command.

Then the consequences of belated preparation—belated through no fault of Gough—became apparent. Campbell, applying to the Commissariat for ten days' supplies with transport to carry them, was answered that he could have neither the one nor the other. With the greatest difficulty he, in the course of forty-eight hours, collected food and carriage for two native battalions, (half a battalion of British troops needed as much transport as two native battalions), and

The 14th Light Dragoons charging

with these—the Thirty-Sixth and Forty-Sixth Native Infantry—he marched from Lahore, on the 10th joining Cureton. On the 13th Gough himself came to Lahore, and on the 15th, being satisfied that Shere Singh would not be tempted to cross the river, he authorised Campbell, should a favourable opportunity present itself, to dislodge the Sikhs from Ramnagar.

On the 16th he began his advance with the main body, though still in the dark upon many points. He wrote on the 15th:

I do not know whether we are at peace or at war, or who it is we are fighting for.

And not till a day or two later was he informed that the contest was not to uphold the authority of the Sikh government against rebels, but to overthrow that government altogether. The situation presents a curious parallel to that in which Wellington found himself before Napoleon's advance in the campaign of Waterloo, (Rait, ii.).

On the 17th he learned that the mutinous battalions from Bannu had joined Shere Singh on the north side of the Chenab. Chattar Singh had not yet done so, but his junction might shortly be expected, for Lieutenant Herbert, who had succeeded Nicholson in command at Attock, while maintaining an obstinate defence, reported that his garrison's temper was uncertain and that he could not hold out much longer. In fact it was pretty clear that Gough's hopes of beating the Sikhs in detail must be abandoned. Within twenty-four hours he learned that, before Campbell could deliver his attack, Shere Singh had withdrawn the bulk of his force at Ramnagar to the north bank of the Chenab, leaving only outposts on the southern bank. Gough, therefore, pressed his march northward, with his whole army, which, with the exception of his two heavy batteries, was now complete. (See list following).

★★★★★★

Cavalry Division: Cureton.
    1st Brigade: Brigr. White—H.M. 3rd D. and 14th L.D.;
        5th and 8th Bengal N.C.
    2nd ,, Brigr. Pope—H.M. 9th Lancers; 1st and 6th
        Bengal N.C.

1st Infantry Division: Gilbert.
    1st Brigade: Brigr. Mountain—H.M. 29th Foot; 30th
        and 56th Bengal N.I.
    2nd ,, Brigr. Godby—2nd Europ. L.I. (102nd); 31st and

70th Bengal N.I.

2nd Infantry Division: Thackwell.

    1st Brigade: Brigr. Pennycuick—H.M. 24th; 25th and
        45th Bengal N.I.

    2nd   „   Brigr. Hoggan—H.M. 61st Foot; 6th and 36th
        Bengal N.I.

    3rd   „   Brigr. Penny—15th, 20th and 69th Bengal N.I.

Artillery:

    6 Horse-batteries (Lt.-Col. Huthwaite)—Lane, Christie,
        Huish, Warner, Duncan, Fordyce.

    3 Field-batteries—Dawes, Kinleside, Austin.

    2 Heavy batteries—Major Horsford.

★★★★★★

So long as Shere Singh lay quietly on the north bank of the Chenab he was on fertile ground, could feed his troops easily, and could await the coming not only of Chattar Singh, but, if the wily old chief could be tempted to throw in his lot against the British, even of Gholab Singh from Kashmir. Obviously, therefore, the sooner Shere Singh were pushed back, the better.

On the 21st Gough came up with Campbell in his camp about eight miles from Ramnagar, and decided, as a preliminary operation, to drive the Sikh outposts across the river and to capture any guns that they might have upon the southern bank. On the night of the 21st, therefore, he pushed forward Colin Campbell with one infantry brigade, Cureton's cavalry division and three batteries of horse-artillery, and at 3 a.m. on the 22nd Gough joined this force in person. As day dawned they came up to Ramnagar and, from the eminence upon which it stands, could observe that the bulk of the Sikh force was in position upon the north bank, but that parties of the enemy were retiring from Ramnagar over the two miles of flat ground that lay between it and the river.

The Chenab at this point is extremely wide from bank to bank, but in the winter the stream is contracted to a narrow channel running in a sandy bed and constantly changing its course. The sand in the bed is everywhere deep, and, however tempting to the eye at a distance, not a surface whereon it is prudent to employ cavalry or artillery. However, the two miles of flat ground were sound enough, and Gough pushed forward Lane's and Warner's troops of horse-artillery, with an escort of White's cavalry, to hurry the retreat of the retiring Sikhs and play

113

upon them as they crossed the ford.

The Sikhs on the north bank thereupon sent cavalry over to protect their comrades, and White, allowing them to enter upon the flat ground, charged them with the Third Light Dragoons and drove them back, but prudently abstained from following them into the broken ground by the river. Thereupon the Sikhs, greatly elated, came forward in greater numbers; but White declined to be tempted into the river-bed, and withdrew, facing about from time to time, and charging when he saw fit opportunity. He had no intention of being drawn under the fire of the Sikh batteries to no purpose.

Unfortunately Lane, in order to cover White's retirement, took his guns too far down into the bed of the river, where one of them stuck fast and could not be brought off except by taking it for some distance along the bed of the river under the full blast of the Sikh batteries on the north bank. It was, therefore, perforce abandoned. Campbell wished to post two battalions under cover to prevent the Sikhs from carrying it off, but Gough disapproved of this.

The Sikhs, in exultation, now pushed further bodies of cavalry across the river, and Gough, taking the direction of the operations into his own hands, ordered Colonel Havelock, a brother of Henry, to charge them with the Fourteenth Light Dragoons. Havelock, wild with excitement, appears to have led his regiment straight against the Sikh reserve of cavalry, which lay in the river-bed, covered by the fire of guns and of hidden infantry. Cureton, with a small escort of native cavalry, galloped forward to stop him, but was shot dead by a bullet through the head before he could reach him. Gough likewise sent an *aide-de-camp* to check Havelock; but that officer was hurrying too fast to be overtaken.

The Fourteenth galloped straight into the trap, with the Fifth Light Cavalry in support, and were not extricated without serious loss. Of the Fourteenth, Havelock, another officer and twelve men were killed, four officers and thirty-one men wounded. The Fifth Light Cavalry lost three officers killed, besides twenty more casualties among the men and forty among the horses. The whole affair cost twelve officers and eighty-four men killed and wounded.

More than half of these casualties were quite unnecessary, and the death of Cureton was a real loss to the army. He was one of the few generals who have risen from the ranks, having served through the whole of the Peninsular War in the Fourteenth Light Dragoons; and it should seem from Colin Campbell's account of the action, (Shadwell, *Life of Lord Clyde*, i.), that Gough would have done much better to leave Cureton to handle his cavalry in his own way. However, the southern bank of the Chenab had been cleared of the enemy; and Gough was able to pitch his camp at Ramnagar, and pursue his operations for forcing the passage of the river. To do so in the face of the Sikh army, occupying a strong position with abundant artillery on the higher bank, was not to be thought of.

But there were other fords farther up the stream, at Garhi-Galla, which was carefully guarded by the enemy, seven miles away, at Khanki and Chak Ali Sher, close to each other five to seven miles farther on, and lastly at Wazirabad, twenty miles above Ramnagar, where there was also a ferry. Gough, therefore, resolved to hold the Sikhs opposite Ramnagar, and to turn their position by a wide flanking movement to his right. The command of the turning column was entrusted to Sir Joseph Thackwell, who had taken over the cavalry division upon the death of Cureton, and had handed his infantry division to Campbell.

The force entrusted to him was White's cavalry brigade, with the Third and Twelfth Irregular cavalry substituted for the Fourteenth Light Dragoons; the Twenty-Fourth and Sixty-First Foot, five-and-a-half native battalions, (4 cos., 22nd, the 25th, 31st, 36th, 46th and 56th Bengal N.I., the original organisation of the brigades seems to have been changed), three troops of horse-artillery, two light field-batteries and two eighteen-pounder siege-pieces. The whole represented about seven thousand men with thirty-two guns. The arrival of the heavy artillery on the 30th completed Gough's arrangements, and Thackwell received his orders to march at midnight.

Gough's instructions gave Thackwell discretionary powers to cross at any ford that he might choose, and to attack, if he could do so with advantage; but, since Garhi-Galla was known to be well guarded, he was directed to move towards Wazirabad, using the ford of Khanki, or that of Chak Ali Sher, if practicable. It was specially enjoined upon him that, unless he could be sure of bringing his troops full and fresh upon the enemy's flank opposite Ramnagar by 1 p.m. at latest on the 1st of December, he should take a second day to complete the movement.

The operation at the outset did not prosper.

The cavalry was all ready to march at midnight, but, the night being very dark, two out of three of Colin Campbell's brigades lost their way to the rendezvous, and wandered about the camp for two hours before they found it. The way lay along narrow roads, where there were any, and over broken ground and heavy sand; and thus the column did not approach the two fords until 11 a.m. on the 1st of December. A staff-officer, who examined that of Chak Ali Sher, reported it difficult for guns and impracticable for pontoons, with signs of quicksands under the farther bank; and he added that the enemy was on the farther side, prepared to resist, and in a position from which the British guns could not easily drive them out. That of Khanki presented much the same difficulties; and in the face of the engineers' reports, Thackwell decided that to cross the river by either ford was impossible, (Wylly, *Military Memoirs of Sir Joseph Thackwell*.) Colin Campbell, to whom the whole enterprise seemed unduly hazardous, was now for returning to Ramnagar; but Thackwell determined to push on to Wazirabad.

There the troops arrived between five and six o'clock in the evening, greatly fatigued after eighteen hours under arms; but Thackwell was rewarded on his arrival by favourable news. He had sent John Nicholson ahead with some irregular horse, and that indefatigable officer had already collected fifteen large boats and staked out two of the fords over the three channels in which the Chenab was then running. There was no sign of an enemy; the Twenty-Fourth, two native battalions and two guns were at once ferried over to make good the passage; and other troops continued to pass in boats all through the night. A regiment of irregular horse rode through the ford; but a second brigade of infantry, while wading over, was stopped by darkness and compelled to bivouac on a sandbank in the bed of the river.

The night was bitterly cold, and no supplies could be brought to the advanced troops, who were fain to wait hungry and shivering for the dawn. But the light came at last, and by noon the whole of the force was safely across the river. Thackwell then sent back his pontoon-train and his two heavy cannon to Ramnagar, under escort of a regiment of native cavalry, two companies of infantry and two guns, with a letter to Gough reporting that he stood on the north bank of the Chenab. At 2 p.m. Thackwell began his march down the right bank in order of battle, traversed about ten miles without seeing a sign of the enemy, and finally halted at dusk at the village of Daurawala. Here he received a message from Gough, saying that he would make every demonstration that he could in order to hold the enemy before Ramnagar, but bidding Thackwell above all things to bring his troops up fresh. Thackwell, accordingly, marched at six next morning, clearing the enemy's detachments from the north bank as he passed, with every intention of falling on the left flank and rear of the Sikhs'

116

main position.

He had reached a point two miles south of the Garhi-Galla ford when he received, in quick succession, three letters, two of them from Gough and one from an officer of his staff. Both of Gough's letters were dated on the preceding day, the first announcing that he should continue his demonstration on the 3rd and try to force a passage; the second, that the enemy was withdrawing from his front but still keeping the fords well protected. The staff-officer gave Thackwell definite orders not to move to the attack, after he had mastered the ford of Garhi, until reinforcements of a brigade of cavalry and Godby's brigade of infantry should reach him.

Thackwell accordingly halted, sent a detachment to hold the ford of Garhi, pushed Nicholson's horse well ahead, occupied four villages in his immediate front, and himself rode down to look to the disposition of the troops guarding the ford. During his absence Nicholson sent in reports of Sikh horse to the front; and, on the general's return, the opening of the Sikh artillery showed him that the enemy was present in force. Shere Singh, in fact, had answered Gough's demonstration by a little demonstration of his own, and slipped away from before him to throw all his strength upon Thackwell.

The villages being surrounded by fields of tall and thick sugar cane, Thackwell withdrew his troops from them and fell back a couple of hundred yards to open ground immediately before the village of Sadullapur. This movement was construed by the Sikhs as a retreat; and Shere Singh, who was present in person, rapidly developed his attack, filling the cane-fields with his infantry, firing heavily from twenty guns, some of them of heavy calibre, and manoeuvring to threaten both of Thackwell's flanks with his cavalry. Thackwell easily drove back the Sikh horse with his own cavalry and horse-artillery, but did not venture to assail the infantry.

The action was therefore continued as a duel of artillery for some two hours, when the Sikh fire slackened, and Thackwell directed his cavalry on the right to charge and capture the guns if they saw a favourable opportunity. But no opening offered itself; and it was not until 3.30 p.m. that Thackwell received a further message from Gough, authorising him to act as he might think best, whether the reinforcements had joined him or not. He then decided that at so late an hour it would be inexpedient to advance to the attack, and the action came to an end.

★★★★★★

Colin Campbell (see *Shadwell*, i.) averred that he twice begged Thackwell's leave to attack with his infantry. Thackwell denied this, and I believe Thackwell. An officer who wished to run back to Ramnagar because the ford at Khanki was impracticable, shows no very enterprising nature.

★★★★★★

Thackwell's casualties did not exceed seventy-six; those of the Sikhs were probably heavier, for many corpses were found in the cane-fields and in the wells of the villages, (Thackwell, The Second Sikh War). But the affair was little more than a skirmish, neither side being willing to close with the other.

Gough was deeply chagrined. He had, he declared, "placed the ball at Thackwell's foot, and Thackwell had declined to kick it." But the main fault lay with Gough himself, for he had been completely outwitted by Shere Singh. True to his promise, Gough had kept his cannon steadily at work all through the 2nd and 3rd; but the Sikhs had withdrawn most of their troops and all but six guns, which were so craftily concealed that the British guns could not silence them. Gough, therefore, was wasting ammunition against half-empty trenches, while Shere Singh had moved off in strength to overwhelm Thackwell; and it is noteworthy that Gough made no attempt, in spite of his professions to Thackwell, to force a passage at Ramnagar. He seems to have had some inkling of the true state of affairs, otherwise he would not have promised further reinforcements to Thackwell and forbidden him to attack without them.

As a matter of fact, the cavalry which should have joined Thackwell by the ford of Garhi-Galla never joined him at all, and only part of Godby's brigade reached him on the morning of the 4th. The ford, in fact, was too deep for them to pass on foot, and the channels were too many to be crossed by pontoons; and Godby was only able to carry his men over the river by using boats which Thackwell had sent down from Wazirabad. The fact seems to reflect upon the work of Gough's staff, but it is certain that the ford has been carefully examined, and that full reports had been sent to Gough. There is, however, nothing more treacherous than a glacier-fed river; and it is likely enough that the fords were never the same for twenty-four hours together.

Such miscarriages as these are the commonplaces of war; but it is certain that Gough was convinced in his own mind that he had given Thackwell full discretion to attack, whether that officer should have received his reinforcements or not, and he intimated as much in his despatch. His good faith cannot be called in question, and, as his staff kept no copies of the orders sent to Thackwell, Gough did not know what he had or had not bidden him to do. All that he did know was that, in Thackwell's place, he would have attacked.

Whether Thackwell should not have thrown all orders to the winds and fallen at once upon Shere Singh is a question that cannot be profitably discussed. Thackwell was an officer of long experience, who had served in the cavalry throughout the Peninsular War, lost an arm at Waterloo, commanded the cavalry under Keane in the first stage of the Afghan War, and under Gough at Maharajpur and at Sobraon. He knew that he was engaged in a very critical operation. He had been told that Gough contemplated pushing across the river at Ramnagar; and, with the Commander-in-chief's orders before him, he might well have concluded that his function was to contain the force opposed to him, while Gough forced the passage.

Gough, on the other hand, considered that it was for him to contain and for Thackwell to attack; and the truth seems to be that Gough was certainly in the dark as to the enemy's movements, and by no means very clear as to his own plans. He considered that an opportunity had been lost; and perhaps he was right. But a commander who desires opportunities to be seized should give a subordinate a free hand.

However, the passage of the Chenab had been won at a trifling cost, and that was, after all, the main point. The Sikhs entrenched before Ramnagar slipped away on the night of the 3rd, abandoning sixty boats and destroying or burying eight guns and a quantity of ammunition. Shere Singh likewise withdrew from before Thackwell at midnight, and Thackwell pushed northward in pursuit with the cavalry under his personal command on the morning of the 4th, but saw no sign of the enemy. Gough, who appears not to have been aware of the withdrawal of the Sikhs from his front until 8 a.m., sent the Ninth Lancers across the ford of Ramnagar to follow them up; but Major Hope Grant, who was in command, though he obtained contact with their rearguard, was unable to press them owing to the density of the jungle.

Grant joined Thackwell that night; and Thackwell on the next day sent his advanced squadrons as far as Dinga, but without overtaking any of the enemy's troops or guns. On the 6th he received orders to form a standing camp at Helan; and on the 7th came news that Shere Singh, reinforced by four regiments and twelve guns from Peshawar, had entrenched himself on the Jhelum between Mong and Rasul.

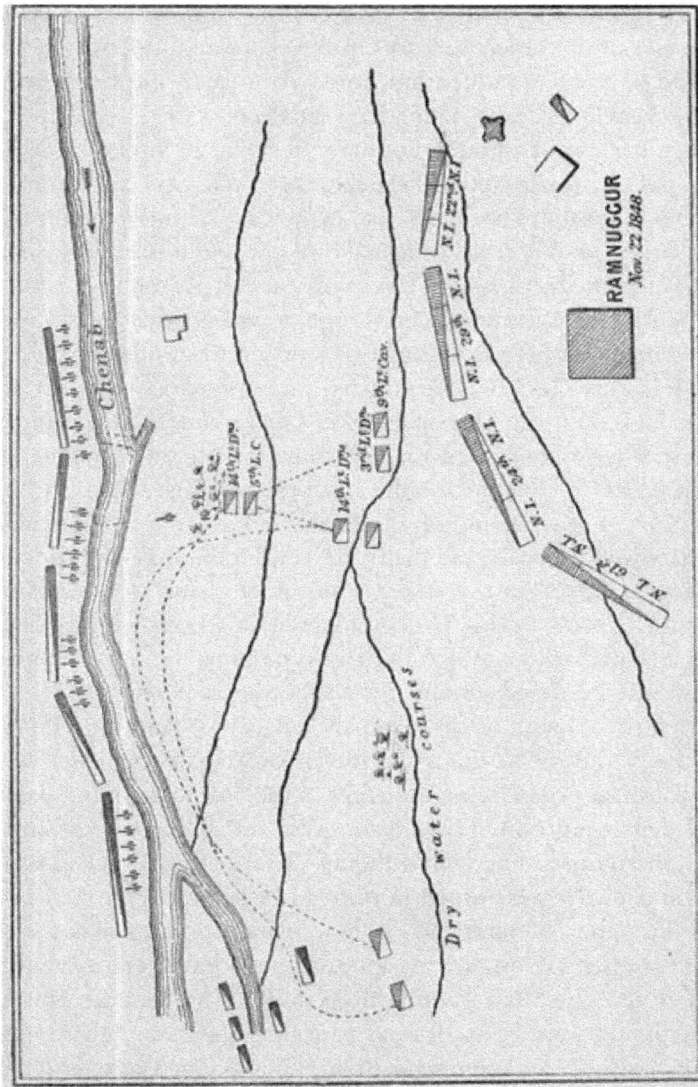

THE COMBAT OF RAMNUGGUR

RAMNUGGUR
Nov. 22 1848.

REFERENCES.

Troops of Horse Artillery accompanied the Cavalry. The remainder of the Artillery was massed in front of the Second Brigade from the right. The position of the abandoned gun is marked in front of the grove.

N.B.—For "22nd" read "2nd Europeans."

But it was impossible for Gough to follow him up with his whole army, because the Commissariat was unable to feed it. Moreover, Dalhousie absolutely forbade further advance beyond the Chenab, "except for the purpose of attacking Shere Singh in his present position," without permission sought and gained from the governor-general. No commander-in-chief could undertake military operations upon such terms, for, if Shere Singh chose to shift his position when Gough reached it, Gough would have to wait for a messenger to go to Ambala, where Dalhousie had taken up his quarters, and to return with, or without, the necessary permission. Indeed, Dalhousie intended that his words should amount to prohibition of any forward movement.

The governor general was not too well pleased with the course of events. He complained that Gough had insisted upon starting before his commissariat arrangements were completed; and this was true; but it was Dalhousie's doing that they had been begun so late, and it was Currie's entreaties that had stimulated Gough to haste, (Rait, ii.). He was annoyed, too, because Gough wished him to fire a royal salute for the passage of the Chenab, which, very reasonably, Dalhousie declined to treat as a great victory. Lastly, over and above Gough's difficulties of transport and supply, Dalhousie reflected, quite truly, that the General's communications were insecure, and that he had no reserve whatever.

Gough himself had doubts whether he were in sufficient strength to attack the Sikhs on the Jhelum until the fall of Multan should have released the troops employed, or to be employed, in the siege, for the reinforcement of the main army, (Burton). Dalhousie took him at his word, and made Gough's further offensive movements contingent upon the capture of Multan. Beyond doubt, if Dalhousie had listened to Gough in the first instance, troops would have been at hand to furnish a reserve, the Commissariat would have been fully equipped, and the siege of Multan—a flagrant blunder—would not have been undertaken.

But it was the governor-general's duty to face facts as they were, not as they might have been, and having faced them he pronounced his judgement. Gough accordingly halted, and made his preparations to concentrate at Wazirabad.

Meanwhile Whish, taking note of the departure of Shere Singh with his troops from Multan, and of the consequent weakening of Mulraj's force, attacked the latter under the walls of the city on the 7th, capturing his position, together with five guns.

★★★★★★

The troops engaged were one horse-battery, the 11th Irreg. Cav., detachments of the 7th Irreg. Cav., H.M. 10th and 32nd Foot, 8th, 49th, 51st and 52nd N.I. Their casualties were 3 killed and 58 wounded.

★★★★★★

On the 25th Whish reoccupied his original station before Multan, and Colonel Cheape, the Chief Engineer, thoroughly reconnoitred the enemy's works against the arrival of the reinforcements from Bombay. These, (one horse-battery, two light field-batteries, 1st Bombay L.C. and Sind Horse; 2 cos. Sappers; H.M. 60th Foot; 1st Bombay Europeans; 3rd, 4th, 9th, 19th Bombay N.I.), arrived at last under the command of Brigadier-General Dundas, on the 22nd of December, having been needlessly delayed for a month by the stickling of the Bombay government over a point of military etiquette. Whish's numbers were thus raised to about fifteen thousand regular troops, besides Edwardes's levies; and on the 26th he issued his orders for an attack on the suburbs to the south-west of the city, so as to clear the ground for the erection of his batteries. The onslaught was delivered at noon on the 27th in four columns, each about one thousand strong, two of them led each by five companies of the Sixtieth and the remaining two by three companies of the Tenth and as many of the Thirty-Second.

It was perfectly successful at a cost of rather more than two hundred casualties. Of these the larger part fell upon the Bombay troops; but the Sixtieth escaped lightly from the extreme skill of the men in taking cover. It is worthy of notice that the Sikhs in this engagement fired shrapnel-shell, showing that they had learned something from their enemies.

On that same evening Whish established three batteries containing altogether thirteen mortars; on the 29th batteries of two twenty-four pounders, six eighteen-pounders and four heavy howitzers were added; and on the 30th five more mortars of large calibre. The fire of these heavy pieces was crushing. On the morning of the 30th the enemy's principal magazine in the citadel was blown up by a shell, and by evening practically every gun had been silenced. By the 2nd of January 1849, two practicable breaches had been made, and on that day Whish gave orders for the storming of the city on the morrow.

The work was entrusted to two columns. The right column, under Brigadier-General Markham, made up of the Thirty-Second Foot, and the Forty-Ninth and Seventy-Second Native Infantry, all of the

The 1st Bombay European Fusiliers storming the breach at the Kooni Boorj at 3 p.m. Jan. 2nd

Bengal Division, was to assault near the Delhi Gate; the left column, consisting of the First Bombay Europeans, (the 103rd), and the Fourth and Nineteenth Bombay Native Infantry, under Brigadier-General Stalker was to assail a breach at an angle of a work named the Khuni Burj. By 2 p.m. the troops were in their appointed places, and at 3 p.m. the signal was given to advance.

Markham's column was led by two companies of the Thirty-Second under Captain Smyth, which, on surmounting the breach, found that the city wall, thirty feet high and quite impracticable, was standing intact within it. Smyth at once decided to retire and fall back upon the main column, which was promptly led by Markham to the other breach by the Khuni Burj. Stalker's column had already entered it, the storming party being composed of three companies of the Bombay Europeans under Captain Leith.

The enemy's fire was kept down by a battery and by the accurate fire of the Sixtieth's rifles. Colour-Sergeant John Bennet was the first to mount the breach, planting his colour on the summit and standing by it until the entire column had passed. The Sikhs had entrenched the breach and broken up the ramparts by traverses, but all resistance was speedily overcome; and the troops streamed into the town in small bodies through a maze of narrow lanes, each party fending for itself and following wherever the flying enemy might lead them.

By nightfall the town had been completely cleared, but the men were scattered in all directions, and it was impossible in the darkness to set up communication between them. What happened during those obscure hours no one has told us; but in the course of the night one of the enemy's powder magazines exploded and destroyed several men. By daylight order was restored; and there now remained only the citadel, containing, as was reckoned, about two thousand men, which was at once closely beset. By the 6th two mortar-batteries were smothering this last stronghold in shells, and Mulraj asked for terms; but, being answered that Whish would hear of nothing but unconditional surrender, he prolonged his resistance.

In the course of the next few days twenty-two more heavy pieces were brought into position, and a sap was begun, with the object of blowing up the counterscarp. The enemy stood manfully to their guns for a time, but on the 18th Mulraj's followers began to desert him; and on the 22nd he surrendered. Between three and four thousand men laid down their arms; and Vans Agnew and Anderson were avenged.

It does not seem that Mulraj's people made a very good fight at

Multan. The assault on the 3rd of January cost only two hundred and fifty casualties, many of which were due to the accident of the explosion, and even so the slain did not exceed seventeen. The Bombay Europeans suffered most heavily, losing four killed and fifty-nine wounded, chiefly, no doubt, among the storming party. Whish seems to have done his work swiftly and resolutely, having abundant force at his disposal. Being an officer of the Indian artillery, who had served at the siege of Bhurtpore, he had experience of such operations; and it is therefore the more surprising that he should have fixed the hour of the assault for three o'clock of an afternoon which was within a fortnight of the shortest day. He must have known that, however rapid his success, night must close down before he could collect his troops after the excitement and disorder of the storming; and that they would inevitably disperse in all directions to plunder and despoil.

It appears to be no exaggeration to say that for twelve hours he utterly lost control of the attacking columns; and it is very clear that they passed their time plundering by the light of torches, and so kindled a certain number of houses, one of which was a powder magazine. In fact, from General Stalker's report, (*Blue Book*, Punjab Papers, 1847–1849), it seems to have been a miracle that there were not many more accidents of the same kind. Fortunately, as is usual in the assault of an Indian fortress, all resistance ceased, practically, as soon as the assailants had made good their footing; but a resolute little band of the enemy might, for all that can be seen to the contrary, have cut them to pieces in detail during the night. The whole proceeding was characteristic of the old school of generals in the Indian Army.

CHAPTER 6

Battles of Chilianwala and Gujrat

The capture of the city of Multan produced its natural reaction upon Dalhousie's plans. Already they had been affected by the news that Attock, since the first week of December, stood in the greatest peril. Gough had written on the 11th that his difficulties of transport, supply and communications were being overcome; and on the 17th the governor-general more or less withdrew his prohibition of an attack upon the enemy on the Jhelum, (Lee-Warner, *Life of Marquis of Dalhousie*, i.).

Gough, during the period of inaction, had made frequent reconnaissances of the Sikh position, but not until the 18th did his headquarters cross the Chenab, Shere Singh having on that day advanced ten thousand men to Dinga, as if to threaten the British communications by way of Wazirabad. The movement was but a feint, for in a few days the Sikhs retired, and on the 29th Gough's headquarters moved forward five miles north of the Chenab to Januki. On that same day an Afghan Army, under the Amir Dost Mohamed in person, joined Chattar Singh before Attock. The garrison, long wavering, lost heart altogether; and Herbert, realising that they would resist no longer, stole away on the night of the 2nd of January, 1849, and left the fortress to its fate.

On the 7th Dalhousie, heartened by the news of the surrender of Multan, wrote to Gough that he would rejoice to hear of a similar blow struck at the Sikhs upon the Jhelum. On the 10th came the news of the fall of Attock; and Major Mackeson, the political officer at Gough's headquarters, strongly urged an immediate attack, before the forces of Chattar Singh should have time to join those of Shere Singh. Gough was nothing loath. He pronounced his army, though it had not been reinforced, perfectly competent to overthrow Shere Singh effectually; and he had already on the 9th moved forward three or four miles to Loah Tibbah. On the 11th he sent Dalhousie his rough plan of attack; on the 12th he marched to Dinga, within eight miles of the Sikh position; and on that evening he summoned his generals and gave them their orders for the fateful morrow.

The Sikhs, once again, as at Aliwal and Sobraon, had taken up a position with a broad river, the Jhelum, in their rear, extending in a concave line from the village of Lakhniwala on their right to that of Rasul on their left, a distance, as the crow flies, of some six miles. Its front was towards the east, so that Rasul formed the northern and Lakhniwala the southern extremity of their array. The Sikh regular troops were distributed in a succession of villages on their right—the south—of this line. The Bannu troops were at Lakhniwala, to the strength of one regiment of horse and four of foot, with eleven guns; a mile to north of them at Chak-Fateh-Shah was Lal Singh with two regiments of horse, ten of foot and seventeen guns; yet another mile to northward at Laliani was Shere Singh, with one regiment of cavalry, nine of infantry, some four thousand irregular horse and twenty guns. Then came the irregular levies, some of them at Mong, in rear of Chak-Fateh-Shah, and thus in second line; and the rest stretching away to the northern extremity at Rasul. The whole were reckoned at some thirty thousand men with sixty-two guns.

In front of the enemy's entrenchments, from Laliani and Lakhniwala and beyond it, ran a line of low rugged jungly heights, sloping gently towards the eastern plain by which Gough would approach it but, to north and west of Rasul, falling down abruptly towards the river on the west in steep bluffs, precipitous cliffs and innumerable ravines. To north of Laliani this ridge abruptly changed its direction from north and south to east and west; the village of Rasul lying hard by the north-eastern extremity, among such a network of ravines as to be almost inaccessible. So far as can be gathered, this ridge of Rasul (as it may be named) was the only portion of the high ground which formed part of the entrenched position. Running as it did, almost at right angles to the main ridge, batteries erected upon it would of course enfilade that main ridge or any enemy advancing to the attack of it.

After making allowance for camp-guards, Gough reckoned that he could bring into action about twelve thousand men and sixty-six guns, (see list following); and with these he marched on the morning of the 13th across a plain so thickly covered with jungle that he bore at first considerably to his right in order to avoid it.

★★★★★★

Cavalry Division: Thackwell.
    1st Brigade: White—H.M. 3rd L.D.; 5th and
        8th Bengal N.C.
    2nd ,, Pope—H.M. 9th Lancers and 14th L.D.; 1st
        and 60th Bengal N.C.

1. Infantry Division: Gilbert.
    1st Brigade: Mountain—H.M. 29th Foot; 30th and
        56th Bengal N.I.
    2nd ,, Godby—2nd Bengal Europeans (H.M. 104th);
        31st and 70th Bengal N.I.

2. Infantry Division: Campbell.
    1st Brigade: Pennycuick—H.M. 24th Foot; 25th and
        45th N.I.
    2nd ,, Hoggan—H.M. 61st Foot; 36th and 46th N.I.
    3rd ,, Penny—15th, 20th and 69th Bengal N.I.

Artillery: Tennant.
    Horse-batteries: Brooke.
        1st Brigade: Grant—Lane's, Christie's and Huish's.
        2nd ,, Brind—Warner's, Duncan's and Fordyce's.
    Foot-batteries: Huthwait.
      3 Field-batteries—Mowatt's, Robertson's and Dawes's.
      2 Heavy-batteries—Maj. Horsford; Capts. Shakespeare
        and Ludlow (each of four 18-pdrs. and
        two 8-in. hows.).

★★★★★★

Before changing his direction upon the village of Chilianwala he halted, and sent his heavy guns to dislodge a Sikh outpost from a mound before that village, which done, he mounted to the roof of a house to examine the enemy's position more closely for himself. The jungle in this quarter was much thinner, though sufficient still to baffle accurate observation; but Gough was in no hurry, for he had not made up his mind whether he should not confine the day's work to a reconnaissance in force, and defer the action until the morrow. It was certain that a frontal attack was out of the question, the left flank of the Sikhs at Rasul being unassailable, and the right protected by dense jungle. It was apparent, too, that the Sikhs had moved forward from their entrenched position; but the ground which they had taken up was too well screened for exact scrutiny; and Gough gave orders for the army to halt and encamp, and for the officers of engineers to go forward and make their report.

The staff was already laying out the ground for the camp, when some Sikh horse-artillery advanced and opened fire upon his outposts. Gough ordered his heavy batteries to the front of Chilianwala village to answer this fire; and the challenge was taken up by a salvo from the whole length of the Sikh line. This revealed the position of the Sikh artillery; and it was evident that, if Gough encamped, the enemy would cannonade him throughout the night. Retreat was not to be thought of. The only course was to fight at once.

It was now about two o'clock, and Gough lost no time in forming his order of battle, while his heavy guns fired steadily upon the enemy's position. On his right was Pope's cavalry brigade with its three horse-batteries; then Gilbert's division with Godby's brigade on the right and Mountain's on the left, and Dawes's field-battery between them; then the two heavy batteries in the centre; then Campbell's division, with Pennycuick's brigade on the right and Hoggan's on the left, with Mowatt's battery between them and Penny's brigade as reserve in rear; then Robertson's half-battery, (three guns had been left with the camp-guard, and the 20th N.I. of Penny's brigade also); and then White's cavalry brigade, with its three horse-batteries, on the extreme left.

In each brigade of infantry the British battalion occupied the centre with a native battalion upon either flank. The whole army was drawn up over against the centre of the Sikh line, which overlapped it upon both flanks, and was apparently about a mile distant from it.

At three o'clock Campbell, who had rather more ground to traverse than Gilbert, received the order to advance. He had decided that the density of the jungle forbade him to control both brigades of his division, so he left Pennycuick in independent command, merely telling the Twenty-Fourth that there must be no firing but that the bayonet must do the work. This done, he galloped away to give his personal direction to Hoggan's brigade. Thereupon Pennycuick strode off at once; but, meeting with dense jungle, was obliged more than once to break from line into echelon of companies in order to take ground to the right. Under such disadvantages the accurate re-formation of the line was difficult, if not impossible; but the battalion, a very strong one of young soldiers, pushed on rapidly, until a belt of still thicker jungle compelled the companies to diminish their fronts and

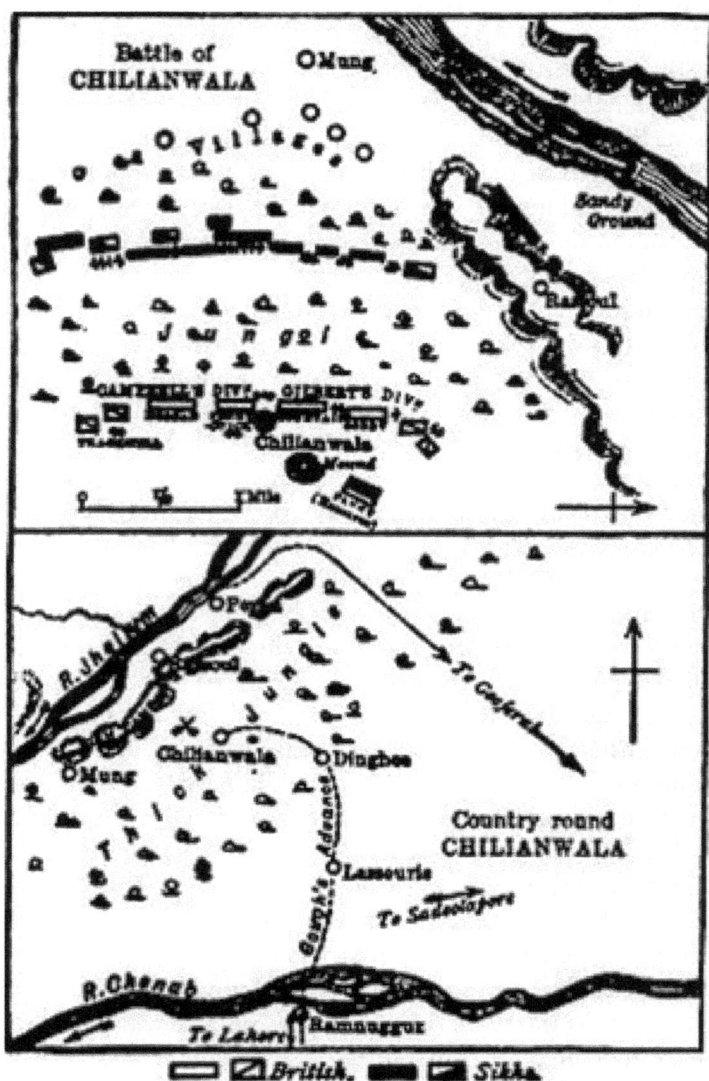

PLAN OF THE BATTLE OF CHILIANWALA,
JANUARY 13th. 1849

struggle through it as best they might. The Sikh batteries had opened fire, making the colonel's word of command inaudible, and stimulating the haste of the men by the crash of the round shot through the branches.

The Twenty-Fourth outstripped Mowatt's battery, masking its fire, outstripped the native battalions on its flanks, and suddenly found itself on clear ground, breathless and disordered, with a natural glacis of grass before them, and at the summit, amid a network of water-pools, the enemy's line and the enemy's batteries. These opened fire upon them with deadly discharges of grape; but without hesitation the Twenty-Fourth made a rush for the guns and disappeared into a cloud of smoke, where, after a short fierce struggle hand to hand, they drove the Sikhs headlong from their pieces.

There is no more dangerous moment than the climax of a successful attack. The men, wild with excitement, scattered and under no control, conceived that their work was done and busied themselves with spiking their trophies, the guns. Meanwhile the Sikhs, perceiving the weak numbers of their assailants, quickly rallied and came forward with reinforcements of infantry to the counter-attack. A shower of bullets smote the dispersed parties of the red-coats, and after a short but furious struggle they were hurled back out of the batteries. The two native regiments on their flanks, though they had not advanced so far, likewise gave way, though a few of each rallied and checked the pursuit of the Sikh cavalry. The brigade was utterly shattered. Pennycuick was shot dead near the guns, and his son, running to his assistance, was killed on his body. In the Twenty-Fourth twenty-one officers and well-nigh five hundred men had fallen, nearly half of them killed; and in the two native regiments nearly three hundred more. The remnant fell back to the point from which they had started, by Chilianwala.

Meanwhile Hoggan's brigade under Campbell's personal direction had likewise advanced, and, though obstructed, albeit in a less degree, by jungle, made its way through it slowly and steadily, supported by Mowatt's battery on the right, and by Robertson's three guns and Brind's three horse-batteries on the left. The fire of these twenty-nine pieces silenced a heavy Sikh battery which would have enfiladed the advance of the brigade, and, thanks to them and to his own control of his troops, Campbell brought up his three battalions in a tolerably well connected line to the open ground beyond the jungle. Here they were faced by a large body of Sikh cavalry and regular infantry, the

Map labels:
- R · I · V · E · R · J · H · E · L · U · M (river)
- TUPAI
- POSITION
- SIKH ENTRENCHED POSITION
- LULLIANEE
- KOT BALOCH
- MOONG
- FUTTEH SHAH KECHUK
- SHAHEEDAWALLA
- LUCKNAWALLA
- J u n g l e

RUSSOOL

Lane

Pope

Godby

Gilbert

Mountain

Penny

Line of Advance from Dinghi

CHILLIANWALLA

MOOJEAWALLA

Pennycuick

Campbell

Eggan

White

BATTLE OF

CHILLIANWALLA

Jan. 13th 1849.

Jungle

Sikh Infantry	1 Christie	
„ Cavalry	2 Dawes	
„ Guns	3 Heavy Guns	
British „	4 Mowatt	
„ Cavalry	5 Robertson	
„ Infantry	6 H.A.	
	7 H.A.	

Direction of Advance.

former, apparently opposite to the Sixty-First, and the latter to the Thirty-Sixth Native Infantry on its right. The Sixty-First charged the cavalry and sent it flying at once, but the Thirty-Sixth were repulsed by the Sikh infantry, which promptly followed them up with two guns. Campbell thereupon changed the front of the two right hand companies of the Sixty-First to the right, and, while the remainder of the battalion was wheeling up to form upon them, these two companies charged and captured the two guns, and by their fire speedily checked the pursuit of the Thirty-Sixth.

The Sikhs thereupon brought up more infantry and two more guns, but these were quickly routed and their guns taken by the Sixty-First. Simultaneously the Sikh cavalry attacked the Forty-Sixth, on the left of the Sixty-First, as it was moving up to the new alignment, but were repulsed. Hoggan's brigade, being now formed on the right flank of the Sikh line, advanced steadily, rolling it up. The Sikh cavalry more than once threatened its flank and rear, causing it to face about; but they were beaten off, and the Sixty-First pressed irresistibly on, charging and capturing thirteen guns, until they had passed the batteries which had repelled Pennycuick, and met Gilbert's left brigade.

Meanwhile the Sikh cavalry over against the British left had not been inactive, but had advanced in considerable strength to turn the left flank. Thackwell, who was with White's brigade, thereupon ordered a squadron of the Third Light Dragoons to charge them, and, if possible, to come down on the flank of the Sikh batteries. The Sikh horse appear to have given way at the very menace of an attack, whereupon the squadrons turned to the more serious business of assailing the batteries. Their advance lay through jungle and stunted trees, beyond which a line of the enemy's infantry was visible at the edge of a low thorny jungle, opening fire at a range of about one hundred yards. The bugle sounded the charge but the native cavalry would not face the musketry, and retired, rallying behind the reserve regiment of their brigade.

Captain Unett's squadron of the Third, on the other hand, crashed straight into the heart of the mass of Sikhs, and was at once desperately engaged. The Sikhs closed in upon their flank, but the Third cut their way through them and pressed on for half-a-mile, when, being much dispersed, they rallied in three or four small parties and charged back through the enemy to their first ground. Of one hundred and six of all ranks forty had fallen; but the Sikhs would not await another such charge and retired off the field. Thackwell then sent a troop of

Captain Unett and his squadron at Chillianwallah

horse-artillery with a squadron of native cavalry for escort, to join Hoggan's brigade, keeping for the present the rest of his division to secure Gough's left flank.

Meanwhile, not many minutes later than Campbell, Gilbert set his division in motion, keeping the whole of it well in hand and under his personal control. His right was protected by Pope's brigade of cavalry; and, seeing a large body of Sikh horse in the direction of Rasul, Pope detached two squadrons each of the Ninth Lancers and of the First and Sixth Light Cavalry with some guns, under Colonel Lane, to cover his right flank. Then, observing more Sikh cavalry in his front, he formed the rest of his brigade in a single line, and advanced on the same front with Gilbert.

Pope was a lieutenant-colonel of native cavalry, who had shown great personal courage in his younger days, but was now past his work, and so infirm that he could not mount his horse without assistance. He knew nothing of wielding large bodies of cavalry, and his ideas of war were apparently limited by his past memories of work as a dashing young squadron-leader. It appears that while bringing his brigade on to its ground he had, partly owing to the density of the jungle, partly from sheer unskilfulness, faced his brigade already in a dozen different directions; and such irresolute handling does not inspire men with confidence.

However, having at last got his line formed, he moved forward at the trot, with no scouts thrown out, until he realised that he was not only masking the fire of his own horse-batteries, but actually overlapping the right of Godby's infantry brigade. Thereupon he reduced the pace to a walk and presently came to a halt, presumably in order to consider what he should do next. It is conjectured that he gave, or meant to give, the word "Threes right"; but a small party of Sikhs, marking that the line was stationary, charged down upon some of the native cavalry; and therewith the word, whatever it may have been (and from such a leader no word could have come as a surprise), was transmuted into "Threes about."Thereupon the whole brigade turned and made for the rear, some with a semblance of order and without undue haste, but the great majority at headlong speed, which grew steadily with the panic of terrified horses and men.

They galloped through Huish's and Christie's batteries, upsetting horses, wagons and guns; and the Sikh horsemen, following in eager chase, cut down Christie himself with many of his gunners, put six guns out of action and carried off four more, two wagons and fifty-three horses. Not until the fugitives had almost galloped over Gough himself were they rallied by the members of his staff.

Through the flight of Pope's cavalry on his right, Gilbert's right flank was wholly uncovered, and he accordingly threw back Godby's brigade somewhat, while Mountain's, with Dawes's battery in line with the skirmishers in front, advanced steadily upon the batteries before the village of Laliani and carried them with the bayonet. Godby's brigade likewise came up shortly afterwards and stormed the batteries in its front with a rush, the Sikh infantry not standing to await their charge. The men had halted and were collecting their wounded, when fire was opened upon them from their rear; and other hostile bodies gathering in upon both flanks surrounded the brigade completely.

Godby, quite unmoved, gave the word "Right about face," and the Hundred and Fourth advanced steadily, loading and firing, while Dawes's battery, which seems to have been everywhere, shattered a body of Sikh cavalry that was bearing down upon Godby's right flank. Godby then ordered a charge of the whole brigade to the rear, and, after a short but violent struggle, cleared himself from his perilous position, having driven off the Sikhs in every direction. Herein he was helped by Penny's reserve brigade, which had been ordered to do the work that Pennycuick had failed to do, but losing its direction, in the jungle, had joined the right of Gilbert's division instead of the right of Campbell's. This fact is significant of the blindness with which the whole action was inevitably fought.

Campbell by this time had joined Mountain, and Thackwell had closed in upon Campbell's left flank, though not in time to prevent the Sikhs from carrying off the guns spiked by Hoggan's brigade. The enemy was in full retreat upon Rasul, suffering somewhat from Lane's guns as they passed; and the battle was over. But Gough had gained little. He could not pursue from want of daylight, and he could not hold his ground from want of water. All ranks were exhausted and maddened with thirst at the close of the action; and many requests came to him for leave to go back for water. Gough's answer was, "I'll be damned if I move till my wounded are all safe"; and not until every wounded man had been carried off did he consent to move back to Chilianwala.

Thus he could not prevent parties of Sikhs from returning and removing under cover of darkness all of their spiked and captured guns excepting twelve light pieces. Thereby not merely the trophies but the fruits of the battle were in great measure abandoned. Moreover,

CHILLIANWALLAH

Gough had lost four of his own guns, and his casualties amounted to over twenty-three hundred killed, wounded and missing. The Sikhs no doubt suffered heavily; but the victory, if victory it could be called, was little to boast of.

The tidings of the battle filled the Indian government with dismay. Dalhousie wrote privately that the conduct of the action was beneath the criticism even of a militiaman like himself; and every pen in India bestirred itself to pass judgement upon it. In England it was set down by the official mind as a disaster; and within forty-eight hours it was determined to send Sir Charles Napier to command the Indian Army, (Lee-Warner, *Life of the Marquis of Dalhousie*, i.).

All of this was a little hysterical. It was generally assumed that Gough's hot Irish blood had, as usual, prompted him to butt his head against a stone wall. This was not so. He had thought out his plan of action, which was sound; and he was prepared, when he started, either to fight or to confine himself to a reconnaissance in force. This being so, he might certainly have marched earlier with advantage, so as to have daylight to follow up his victory, if victory he should win; but that he could have gained any knowledge of the Sikh position without a reconnaissance in force seems extremely doubtful. That, in the actual circumstances, he could have deferred a general action, seems impossible.

So he decided to fight, and began with an hour's cannonade, first of his heavy guns only, then of all of his artillery, before launching his infantry to the attack. And here it is to be noticed that the heaviest of the casualties did not fall upon Pennycuick's brigade, which counted altogether just under eight hundred killed and wounded, of which five hundred belonged to the Twenty-Fourth. It was Mountain's victorious brigade which suffered most severely, the Twenty-Ninth being the battalion that escaped most lightly, (the casualties were: 29th, 241; 30th N.L, 285; 56th N.I., 316).

It seems certain, therefore, that, if the Twenty-Fourth had been adequately supported by the two native regiments upon either flank, their sacrifices would not have been made in vain. On the other hand Pennycuick, who was a gallant and impetuous officer, appears to have hurried his men forward with undue haste, and without waiting for the support of the artillery. But here the question arises, why did not Campbell exert the same control over Pennycuick as over Hoggan? His answer was that the jungle prevented him; but Gilbert had the same difficulty to contend with, and mastered it successfully. The truth seems to be that Colin Campbell, who had only for a short time commanded a division, had not yet risen quite to the height of his new duties.

He handled Hoggan's brigade in a masterly fashion, and accomplished great things at a cost of well under three hundred casualties in the three battalions; but herein he was materially assisted by Brind's batteries of horse-artillery on his left. If he had bestowed the same supervision over Pennycuick's brigade and looked to the careful support of its advance by the guns attached to the division, matters would no doubt have fallen out very differently. But Campbell gave apparently no orders except to tell the Twenty-Fourth that "there must be no firing but that the bayonet must do the work."

The failure of the cavalry on the right was a misfortune which Gough could not have foreseen; but, if it was he who was responsible for the appointment of Pope to the command of the brigade, then he deserves no sympathy. No man who knew the alphabet of cavalry-tactics would have moved the whole of his squadrons forward in line, without any support; and it is very obvious that Pope, incompetent and ignorant at the best of times, was absolutely unfit, physically, for active service. To place good regiments, and both the Ninth Lancers and Fourteenth Light Dragoons were good regiments, under the command of such a man, was like placing valuable porcelain in the hands of a child. The casualties of Pope's brigade in this unhappy affair were trifling, but the disgrace is not even now wholly forgotten.

On the whole, however, considering all the circumstances together, it seems that Gough has received far more censure for Chilianwala than he merited. War is a tricky game; and there never yet was a battle in which the commander-in-chief's plans were not in some measure brought to naught. The difficulties of a fight under cover of thick jungle are very great, and chief among these is that of ensuring concerted action between the various units engaged. To gain this end above all things time is necessary. There must be no hurrying, or at any rate in theory there should be none. But two circumstances militated against a leisurely and methodical attack. The first was that Gough had allowed himself barely two hours' daylight; and the second was Campbell's directions to the Twenty-Fourth to trust to the bayonet only. When men are falling fast under a heavy fire and are forbidden to answer it, a leader may well hasten his men on as the only chance of getting them forward at all.

So, apparently, did Pennycuick; with the result that the Twenty-Fourth alone followed him, that they gained their objective too soon, and that they were overwhelmed by a counter-attack before any support could reach them upon either flank. Whether it be a line of divisions extending for miles, or a line of companies extending for yards; whether the operation be one that lasts for minutes and hours or for days and weeks, the problem of co-ordination in attack and the penalties for failing in its solution remain always the same.

It was well that Gough had taken care to collect his wounded for, before any movement could be made on the morning after the battle, the rain came down, and for three days fell incessantly, turning the ground into a sea of impassable mud. During this interval the army of Chattar Singh joined that of Shere Singh in his entrenched position at Rasul; and, when the weather cleared, Gough decided that it would be impolitic to attack until he should be reinforced by the troops from Multan. He, therefore, decided to sit still, detaching two regiments of native cavalry under Lieutenant Hodson to Wazirabad, to guard against any attempt of the enemy to cross the Chenab. Dalhousie, it seems, was entirely of the same mind as Gough, (Lee-Warner, *Life of the Marquis of Dalhousie,* i.); but in any case the general was firm in abiding by his resolution.

The fall of Multan was imminent, and meanwhile there was no occasion for extreme haste. In the barren country on the Jhelum the Sikhs could not long subsist; and as early as on the 25th of January, Mackeson received intelligence which pointed to their early movement upon Gujrat. Shere Singh was, in fact, uneasy. He knew that shortly he must withdraw from Rasul, but was unwilling to do so while Gough remained watching him. He was, in fact, in much the same situation as Massena before Torres Vedras, and at last, on the 2nd of February, he left the Bannu troops, some ten thousand men with twenty-seven guns, to hold the entrenchments at Rasul, and with the remainder of his force marched away to eastward.

Then, like Massena, Shere Singh used every wile to lure Gough to a pitched battle. He made first for Khori and thence moved southward upon Dinga, as if to threaten Gough's communications. On the 12th he even made strong demonstrations of attack. Gough was not to be beguiled. He met the menace by pushing forward a few squadrons of cavalry and bided his time, knowing that he could foil any attempt of the enemy to cross the Chenab. Major Mackeson, the political agent at head-quarters, now became urgent for immediate action; but Gough was not to be hurried. On the 13th Brigadier-General Cheape arrived with a few squadrons of irregular cavalry from Multan, showing that Whish was near at hand; and on the 14th intelligence came in that the

Sikh Army had wholly evacuated Rasul and taken up a position at Gujrat, with intent, as they proclaimed, to march on Lahore.

Then at last, on the 15th, Gough broke up his camp and struck southward twelve miles to Lasuri, thus bringing his army nearer than that of the Sikhs to the fords of the Chenab and making sure of his junction with Whish, who was now approaching Ramnagar. By Gough's orders Whish pushed forward the Fifty-Third, a native battalion, two regiments of irregular cavalry and four guns, to reinforce Hodson at Wazirabad; and meanwhile Gough turned eastward by short marches, on the 16th to Pakha Masjid, on the 17th to Kunjah, from which point the enemy was visible about Gujrat, and on the 18th to Trikha. All these movements were made in order of battle, so that the Sikhs were kept in constant apprehension of attack. On the 18th Whish arrived at headquarters; on the 19th Dundas's brigade, marching from Ramnagar, came up on Gough's left; on the 20th the main army advanced to Shadiwal, where Markham's brigade joined it; and Gough, having at last under his hand a force of twenty-four thousand men with ninety-six guns, was ready to strike a decisive blow.

★★★★★★

Gough's Army—21st February 1849.

Cavalry Division: Thackwell.

> 1st Brigade: Lockwood—H.M. 14th L.D.; 1st Bengal
> L.C., detachments of 11th and 18th Irreg. Cav.
> 2nd ,, Hearsey—3rd and 9th Irreg. Cav.
> 3rd ,, White—H.M. 3rd L.D. and 9th Lancers; 8th
> Lt. Cav., Sind Horse, 2 troops horse-artillery.

1st Infantry Division: Whish.

> Hervey's Brigade: H.M. 10th Foot; 8th and 52nd N.I.,
> 1 co. pioneers, 1 troop of horse-artillery.
> Markham's Brigade: H.M. 32nd Foot; 51st and
> 72nd N.I.; 2 troops horse-artillery; Dawes's light
> field-battery. 2 troops of horse-artillery in reserve.
> Reserve: Hoggan—5th and 6th N.L.C.; 45th and 69th N.I.;
> 1 Bombay light field-battery.

2nd Infantry Division: Gilbert.

> Penny's Brigade: 2nd Europeans (104th); 31st and
> 70th Bengal N.I.
> Mountain's Brigade: H.M. 29th Foot; 30th and 56th
> Bengal N.I.

3rd Infantry Division: Campbell.
    Carnegy's Brigade: H.M. 24th Foot; 25th Bengal N.I.
    Mcleod's   ,, H.M. 61st Foot; 36th and 46th Bengal N.I.;
              2 light field-batteries.
    Dundas's ,, H M. 60th Rifles; 1st Bombay Europs.
           (109th); 3rd and 19th Bombay N.I., 1 Bombay
           light field-battery.
Heavy Artillery:
    Ten 18-pounders.
    Eight 8-in. howitzers.

★★★★★★

The Sikhs were drawn up about a mile to south of Gujrat in the form of a crescent, with both flanks slightly refused, facing to the south. In the centre were arrayed their regular infantry with their right resting on the dry bed of the Dwara, and their left on the flowing stream of the Katela, which runs into the Chenab about a mile below the battlefield. The space between these two channels measured roughly six thousand yards, and was covered by two or three fortified villages behind which the battalions were drawn up, with fifty-nine guns in the intervals between them. On either flank stood their cavalry, Dost Mohamed's Afghan horse being on the right. The total force was reckoned at sixty thousand men. Gough's plan was to contain their left centre and left with two brigades of cavalry; to throw his right wing against the enemy's right centre and force it back from the Dwara, and then, having thus ensured the passage of his left wing across the Dwara, to wheel up that left wing and crush the Sikh right centre between two fires.

Accordingly Lockwood's and Hearsey's cavalry brigades, with one troop of horse-artillery, formed his extreme right, from the Katela westward. On their left was Whish's division, Hervey's brigade in front and Markham's in second line; on the left of Whish stood Gilbert's division, Penny's brigade on the right and Mountain's on the left, and on the left of Mountain were the heavy guns. (Burton places Mountain's brigade west of the Dwara, and in his plan shows it first to west and later to east of it. Gough's despatch says plainly that Gilbert's division was on the right—east—of the Dwara).

Then the line was broken by the Dwara, on the western bank of which was Campbell's division, Carnegy's brigade on the right, McLeod's in the centre, Dundas's on the left, with Hoggan's Reserve in rear. On the left flank was White's cavalry-brigade under the per-

BATTLE OF GUJRAT

sonal direction of Thackwell. Allowing for camp-guards and the like, Gough brought into action about twenty thousand men.

The morning of the 21st of February broke calm and cloudless. Soon after dawn the British were in array, and old Gough, conspicuous in his white fighting coat, rode down the line from right to left amid a roar of cheering. The Sikhs had taken up their positions early, so that there was no dust. The plain was open, sprinkled with villages and chequered by patches of cultivation but unscreened by jungle, and behind it loomed up the white chain of the Himalayas and the peaks of eternal snow. For nearly two miles the army strode forward and then the Sikh guns opened fire, prematurely, betraying alike the position and the range of their guns.

Halting his line just in safe ground, Gough pushed his batteries forward, under cover of skirmishers; and at nine o'clock all, except two reserve-batteries, opened fire, the lighter pieces at six hundred, the heavier at eight hundred to a thousand yards. The Sikh guns answered them with their usual rapidity and precision and not without effect, but the two reserve-batteries soon saw and seized an opportunity to enfilade one of the Sikh batteries, (Brigadier-General Tennant's Report, *Blue Book*), and to silence it. This was only a beginning. For two hours and a half the cannonade continued with overwhelming violence; and the Sikh fire became feebler as gun after gun was dismounted and group after group of the gunners was destroyed.

Meanwhile the Sikh horse opposite to Gough's right had come into action early, advancing first in heavy masses upon the front of his cavalry. Hearsey, who commanded the two cavalry brigades in that quarter, willingly accepted the challenge, countering the movement chiefly by skilful use of his horse-artillery; and then the Sikhs endeavoured long and persistently to turn his right flank. Again and again Hearsey foiled them by skilful handling of his squadrons, but the enemy gave him no chance of closing with them; and this incessant manoeuvring to the right led his force further and further from the line of the infantry on his left, until at length the flank of the infantry was exposed. Hearsey sent back Lockwood's brigade to protect it; and the Sikhs then tried to cut Hearsey's own brigade off from Lockwood. They were again thrown back by the guns of the horse-artillery; and then the two parties suddenly realised that the din of the main battle had moved away to northward, and the Sikh horse made off with Hearsey in pursuit.

By noon Gough decided that his cannon had fulfilled its task, and

BATTLE OF GUJRAT

deploying his infantry ordered a general advance, still covered by the artillery. He was, however, cautious enough to direct Gilbert to push forward some light troops to force the Sikhs to disclose their position; and, when Gilbert's two batteries moved on with them, they drew down a very heavy and well directed fire from the Sikh batteries on either flank of the village of Bara Kalra. Gough's heavy guns, which were handled with little less activity than the lighter pieces, promptly came up to silence them; and, since the village seemed to be unoccupied, Gilbert directed a party of infantry to take possession of it. These were met by so staggering a fire of musketry from the loopholed walls that they could make no progress, and Gilbert was fain to order up the Hundred and Fourth to their support.

The village was held by some of the finest of the Khalsa troops, and the fighting was obstinate and bloody; but the Hundred and Fourth were not to be denied, and after a stern struggle drove the defenders out. The Sikh guns in rear of the village now opened impartially upon friend and foe; and the defeated Sikh infantry, rallying when they realised how few were their assailants, returned to the counter-attack. The situation was critical, when some guns of Fordyce's horse-battery, which had fallen back to replenish with ammunition, galloped up and, with a few rounds of grape, added to the volleys of the Hundred and Fourth, checked the onslaught of the enemy, who slowly and sullenly retired.

Simultaneously the Tenth Foot and Eighth Native Infantry of Hervey's brigade attacked the village of Chota Kalra, further to the right. Here again the resistance was stubborn; and the menace of the Sikh cavalry on the right flank compelled Hervey to take ground to the right and to throw back his third battalion in echelon to his right rear. Markham's brigade, however, came forward to fill the gap, and Hervey, with the help of Mackenzie's and Anderson's horse-batteries, mastered the village and threw the enemy back.

Campbell's division on the left advanced without firing a shot, the guns having cleared all before them. There was one point where the Dwara made a bend almost in the same straight line with the Sikh front and where they had infantry and heavy guns in position; but these were driven out and silenced by enfilading fire from the British cannon. On the extreme left Thackwell, even as Hearsey, was threatened with the turning of his outer flank by the Sikh cavalry; but Duncan's and Huish's horse-batteries checked the enemy in front, and the Sind Horse, with a squadron of the Ninth Lancers, repelled the flanking attack by a brilliant charge.

The general advance of the infantry turned the retreat of the Sikhs into a flight. They were thoroughly routed as they had not been since Aliwal, and, throwing away their arms, they dispersed in every direction. Thackwell pressed on rapidly in pursuit to cut the fugitives off from Jhelum, and did not cease until he was twelve miles beyond Gujrat, and the horses of his two batteries could trot no more. Hearsey, vying with his chief, continued the chase for fifteen miles beyond Gujrat, and did not return to camp until ten o'clock at night. Darkness gave the enemy a short respite; but, at dawn of the 22nd, Gilbert with his own division, Fordyce's and Dawes's batteries, the Fourteenth Light Dragoons and the Eleventh Irregular Cavalry, began the hunt anew north-westward, while Campbell was sent northward towards Bhimbar, whither a large body of Sikhs were supposed to have fled.

Campbell returned on the 25th having found no trace of the enemy. Gilbert, moving by Sikri Wala and Puran to Naurangabad, heard there on the 24th that the fugitives were in the act of passing the Jhelum, and hastened with his mounted troops to the ferry, to arrive just too late. A host of Sikh irregulars, some twenty thousand strong, was seen on the opposite bank, but they were out of his reach. Hearsey joined him with his brigade in the evening; but Gilbert was for the present brought to a standstill.

Since the battle Gilbert had traversed a distance of over fifty miles in seventy-two hours, and it is probable that in that exhausted country there was little forage for his transport-cattle. In any case he seems to have halted for three days, when, leaving a regiment of native cavalry to watch the enemy, he on the 27th marched to Sukhlajpur, and, with a small escort of all three arms, set himself to find a ford over the Jhelum. He discovered one which was hardly practicable for infantry; and occupied an island between two channels of the river in some force, having noticed that the enemy were in some strength on the opposite bank. But his mere presence was enough to alarm the Sikhs into further flight; and, having crossed the Jhelum on the 28th, he steadily continued the pursuit.

By the 8th of March he was within thirty miles of Rawal Pindi, where the Sikhs, some sixteen thousand strong, had halted. On that day Shere Singh, Lal Singh and some four hundred followers came in, bringing with them the British prisoners that had been captured at Peshawar and Attock; and on the 9th Shere Singh returned to Rawal Pindi to arrange for unconditional submission. Gilbert, however, pursued his march, receiving the surrender of odd parties and chiefs on the 10th and 12th, and the final surrender of the whole at Rawal Pindi on the 14th. In all there were delivered up twenty thousand stand of arms and forty-one guns; and the power of the Sikhs was finally broken.

It remained to drive the levies of Dost Mohamed from the province of Peshawar, and Gilbert lost no time over it. Starting on the 15th of March, he was on the 16th at Wah, within thirty miles of Attock, where he heard that the bridge of boats at that point was still standing and that the fortress itself was occupied by Afghan troops. Realising the importance of securing this bridge he started upon a forced march on the evening of the 16th, reached Shamsabad at sunrise, and, pushing on with his cavalry and artillery only, reached Attock half-an-hour before noon of the 17th, the guns coming up an hour and a half later. He found the fort of Attock evacuated, and the Afghan rear-guard in the act of crossing the bridge; but his troops had hardly shown themselves before the bridge was hastily broken up, many of the boats floating down the river.

Upon the opposite bank the Afghans were drawn up in force with batteries in position; but they were careful to move off before Gilbert's guns arrived. On the 19th Gilbert passed the river with the whole strength of his column, and on the 21st he entered Peshawar unresisted. The Afghan army had evacuated the place two days before, and fled, rather than retreated, through the Khyber pass. Thus the last work of the campaign was brilliantly done. The victory of Gujrat came as a very timely answer to Gough's many detractors. Every pen in India had, after Chilianwala, been busy in decrying him, and dozens of officers, many of them unworthy to clean his spurs, had pointed out in the press how much better they could have managed things in his place.

The Europeans in India have always been afflicted with a plague of writing, and at this time, and for some years past, they had developed the more alarming symptom of printing their writings. Some of these scribes were able men, as, for instance, Henry Durand and Henry Lawrence; a few had some literary gift; all were consumed by vanity of their literary powers, and not a few by sheer jealousy and spite.

******

The last, or nearly the last, of this school of pretentious Anglo-Indian writers was Colonel Malleson. I know no historical, or pseudohistorical, writings more inaccurate, slovenly and untrustworthy than his.

******

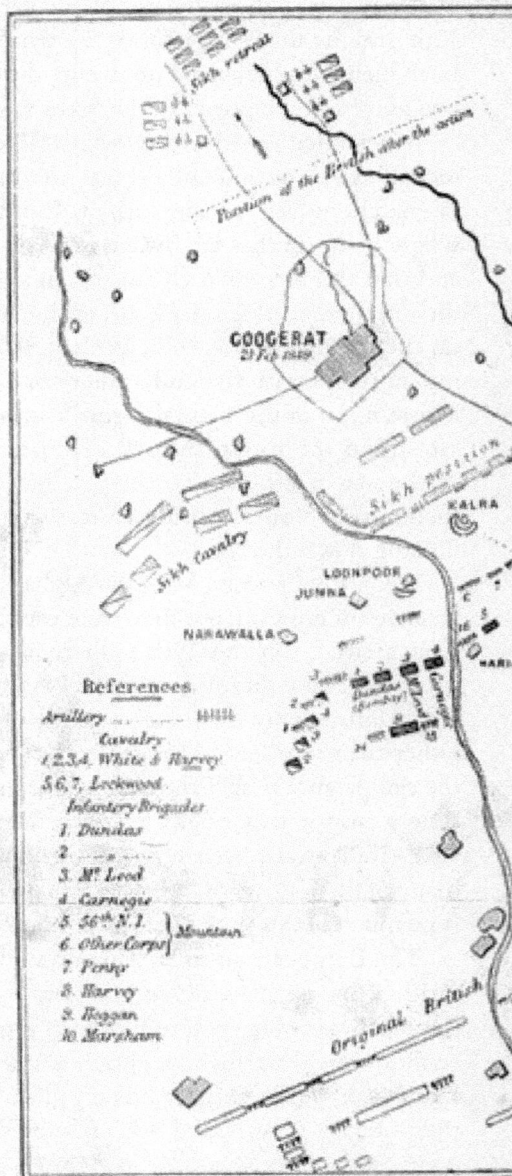

GOOGERAT
21 Feb 1849

KALRA

Sikh retreat

Portion of the British after the action

Sikh position

Sikh Cavalry

LOONPOOR
JUNNA
NARAWALLA
HARI

Original British

References

Artillery ....
Cavalry
1,2,3,4. White & Harvey
5,6,7. Lockwood

Infantry Brigades.

1. Dundas
2. ....
3. M? Leod
4. Carnegie
5. 56th N.I.
6. Other Corps
7. Penny
8. Harvey
9. Hoggan
10. Markham

} Mountain

THE BATTLE

The troops and batteries of Artillery in the above

1. Huish.	5. Robertson.
2. Duncan.	6. Lane (previously 14).
3. Blood.	7. Day.
4. Ludlow.	8. Dawes.

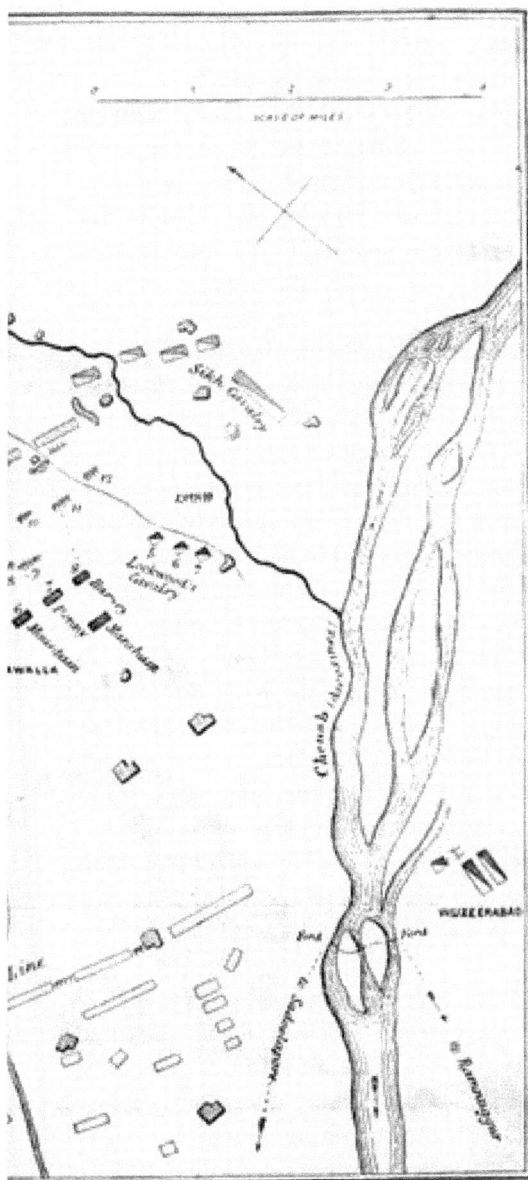

SCALE OF MILES

Sikh Cavalry

Lockwood's Cavalry

Chenab (Chundrabhaga)

WUZEERABAD

Ford

Ford

OF GOOGERAT.

Plan were commanded by the following officers :—

9. Horsford.
10. Fordyce.
11. Anderson.
12. Mackenzie.

13. Warner.
14. See No. 6.
15. Kinloside.
16. Shakspeare.

Nothing more injurious to discipline can be conceived; and it can hardly be doubted that this criticism of seniors by junior officers played its part in the general demoralisation of the Indian army. Yet the practice was not condemned by the Indian government. In fact it seems actually to have been encouraged by the promotion of those who thus showed their literary powers; and it may be pleaded in extenuation that writing is, in a general way, less mischievous than drinking. But old George the Third was justified in his opinion, written nearly seventy years before, that a commercial company was quite unfit to be in charge of an army.

Gough, though bitterly hurt by these incessant attacks, would never condescend to notice them, thereby showing himself much greater than Colin Campbell and Charles Napier. Yet they added considerably to his difficulties, and were a constant source of worry and irritation. Not less severely was he tried by the incessant interference of the political agents. But fortunately he was endowed with great tenacity and very remarkable moral strength and courage. He had thought out the plan that he should follow after Chilianwala, and nothing could turn him from it. He was not going to be led northward by Shere Singh into the barren and difficult country beyond the Jhelum, where the war might be endlessly prolonged. He would do what Pompoedius failed to do with Marius, compel Shere Singh to come down and fight upon Gough's chosen ground and upon Gough's own conditions. With indomitable patience he bided his time, brushing away the political agents who were perpetually buzzing about him with unsolicited advice, (Rait, ii.), and he had his will. It is surely idle to contend that such a man, who moreover, as has been seen, held the soundest views upon all strategical questions, was not only a competent but a distinguished commander.

It remains to consider him as a tactician, and, if he be judged by his last and most successful battle, he must certainly receive his meed of praise. At Gujrat he had for the first time an army of respectable strength and an artillery superior to the enemy's; he used all three arms to the best advantage, and he won a crushing victory at no great cost of life. His casualties did not exceed ninety-six killed and just over seven hundred wounded; but these losses were heavier than he had expected, though through no fault of his. If Gilbert had not been deceived by the peaceful aspect of Bara Kalra he would have turned his heavy guns on to the village and have mastered it with little difficulty. As things were, the storming of the little stronghold cost Penny's brigade three hundred and fifty casualties, of which one hundred and fifty fell upon the Hundred and Fourth, and nearly as many upon the Thirty-First Native Infantry. Hervey's brigade, which attacked Chota Kalra, escaped with no more than one hundred and seventy killed and wounded.

The artillery, who really did the brunt of the work, lost rather over one hundred of all ranks; but among these were no fewer than twenty-nine out of the ninety-six slain in the entire army. The plan of attack was precisely the same as at Chilianwala, but at Gujrat the action of the various units was properly co-ordinated under Gough's own eye, which could not exert the same control at Chilianwala owing to the jungle. In fact the impossibility of overlooking his force had been the cause of the heavy losses at all Gough's previous battles against the Sikhs; and it is worth while to consider whether, in these circumstances, he gave sufficiently clear instructions to his subordinate commanders.

Harry Smith's strictures upon the commander-in-chief's omission to impart his plans to his divisional generals at Ferozeshah have already been quoted. At Sobraon, however, he admitted that every general and commander received full and detailed instructions, though he considered that his own place of attack had been wrongly chosen for him. Hardinge, quite independently of Smith, made much the same criticism. Gough, he wrote:

> . . . . . . has no capacity for administration. He is at the outposts wonderfully active, but the more important points, which he dislikes, of framing proper orders and looking to their execution are much neglected.

This defect, if it were present, points to the probability that Gough had no very efficient staff at his disposal; and this probability is confirmed by the fact that the staff kept no copies of the orders sent to Thackwell when he was sent off in independent command across the Chenab. But it seems to have been a real weakness with Gough that he could not resist taking personal command of small bodies of troops for trifling operations, when he had much better have left matters in the hands of his subordinates, (Shadwell, *Life of Lord Clyde*, i.). It is not an uncommon failing, but it is a serious one; for good administration, whether military or civil, consists in the wise delegation of authority; and a commander-in-chief who insists on doing everything himself is sure of bad mishaps because he cannot be everywhere. This is probably the explanation of Harry Smith's criticism after Ferozeshah. As the result of that action Gough seems to have mended his ways.

But the harsh judgement passed upon Gough, and the wild talk about his fiery Irish temperament, rest chiefly upon the number of his casualties. These were not really excessive, though they seemed to be so because they fell with disproportionate severity upon his British troops. That they were heavy was due to a cause which has not, as it seems to me, been sufficiently emphasised. He had to encounter good infantry as well as good artillery. Much is made of the skill, gallantry and devotion of the Sikh gunners, and let them be duly honoured. Yet these qualities were equally shared by the Mahratta gunners, who had always stood until they were bayoneted by their pieces. But, in rear of the guns, the Mahratta infantry made little or no resistance, unless it were at Maharajpur; and therefore, when their batteries had been stormed, the fight was virtually over.

The Twenty-Fourth would have been victorious at Assaye or at Deig. But the Sikh infantry fought as obstinately as the Sikh artillery, and the troops, after taking the Sikh batteries, had to face and quell the Sikh musketry. This was something quite new in Indian warfare; and even newer and more disquieting was the Sikh practice of meeting attack by counter-attack. For such work Gough needed in every action as strong an army as he commanded at Gujrat, and the more so as he was almost invariably inferior in number and weight of cannon. Lines of assault were sufficient to push the Sikhs off their ground, but columns were needed to make the success decisive. The Sikhs owed their disaster at Sobraon mainly to their madness in fighting with their backs to a river.

Altogether Gough deserves far more honour than has hitherto been accorded to him. He was no wild Irishman, but a good, sound scientific soldier, with nothing specially Irish about him except his boiling courage. His men adored him. Who would not have adored a chief who had ridden out alone into the thick of a heavy cannonade in order to draw fire away from his troops? In England the revulsion of feeling in his favour after Gujrat was immediate and generous, as it should have been. He was not the first commander who had won his crowning victory when his recall was on its way to him; but at least his successor, Sir Charles Napier, was worthy of high station, in marked contrast to the incompetent Admiral Pigot who superseded Rodney in 1782 after the Battle of The Saints. Unfortunately, owing to the hysterical despatches of Dalhousie, Napier's commission ordered him to assume the command in-chief immediately upon landing, which practically compelled Gough to resign.

Napier behaved generously enough, saying that nothing would please him better than that Gough should order him to return home. Dalhousie also directed that during the rest of his stay in India Gough should be treated with his old honours as commander-in-chief, and he omitted no opportunity of showing him personal deference and respect. Yet the old man could not but feel deeply hurt that he should have been so hastily condemned. A viscountcy and the thanks of Parliament did something to comfort him; and an enthusiastic reception upon his arrival in England completely healed his wounded spirit.

Finally the Duke of Wellington, who though past fourscore years of age still weighed his words, at a dinner at the United Service Club, spoke of Gough as:

.... affording the brightest example of the highest qualities of the British soldier.

Such eulogy from such a man should keep sweet the memory of gallant old Hugh Gough in the British Army.

For the rest, the Punjab was annexed to the British dominions in India, and placed under the government of a board of three, two of them being John Lawrence and his brother Henry. Under them a number of specially chosen officers raised Sikh regiments of horse and foot, and worked indefatigably to reduce the chaos of the Sikh states to order. Much of their work was stern, for the country swarmed with masterless soldiers who were little better than *banditti*; and there is a curious picture of John Nicholson, whose nature revolted from taking human life, schooling himself to severity by holding his courts under a tree from which dangled the corpses of the condemned.

Such an example shows that, while there was necessarily justice without mercy at the outset, there was no unthinking inhumanity; and the ultimate result proved the high capacity of the British officer for administration. Nor is such capacity confined to the Indian Army, for it was strikingly manifested in the twentieth century in the Soudan. To dwell longer upon this subject in these pages is impossible; and yet no higher testimony can be brought forward to the ability, the broad, strong sense and the high moral spirit of the British officer.